MEDICAL PRACTICE MANAGEMENT

Body of Knowledge Review

Second Edition

VOLUME 2

Financial Management

Medical Group Management Association
102 Inverness Terrace East
Englewood, CO 80112-5306
877.275.6462
mgma.com

Medical Group Management Association® (MGMA®) publications are intended to provide current and accurate information and are designed to assist readers in becoming more familiar with the subject matter covered. Such publications are distributed with the understanding that MGMA does not render any legal, accounting, or other professional advice that may be construed as specifically applicable to an individual situation. No representations or warranties are made concerning the application of legal or other principles discussed by the authors to any specific factual situation, nor is any prediction made concerning how any particular judge, government official, or other person will interpret or apply such principles. Specific factual situations should be discussed with professional advisors.

PRODUCTION CREDITS
Publisher: Marilee E. Aust
Composition: Glacier Publishing Services, Inc.
Cover Design: Ian Serff, Serff Creative Group, Inc.

LIBRARY OF CONGRESS CATALOGING-IN-PUBLICATION DATA

Financial management.
    p. ; cm. — (Medical practice management body of knowledge review (2nd ed.) ; v. 2)
    Includes bibliographical references and index.
    ISBN 978-1-56829-331-8
  1. Medical offices—Finance. I. Medical Group Management Association,. II. Series.
  [DNLM: 1. Financial Management—organization & administration. 2. Practice Management, Medical. W 80 F489 2009]
    R728.F558 2009
    610.68′1—dc22

                                                              2008044467

Printed in the United States of America
10 9 8 7 6 5 4 3 2

Contents

Preface

WHILE BUDGETS AND BUDGETING LOOK TO THE FUTURE, accounting looks at past events to generate financial statements and assess an organization's operating performance. Financial management also requires the understanding of various financial statements, including the balance sheet, which allows managers to take a snapshot of what the practice owns and owes, and income and cash flow statements.

In its broadest sense, financial management includes four areas that a practice manager must understand to successfully operate a medical group:

1. Generating income;

2. Controlling expenses;

3. Budgeting and planning; and

4. Tax and regulatory agency compliance.

◢ Generating Income

Payer and patient collections largely drive income. Medical revenues are based on the collections that the practice derives from providing clinical services. Collections arise by billing insurers for the services rendered, and the practice receives payment based on fee schedules, payment methodologies (resource-based relative value scale), or on contracted rates.

◼ Controlling Expenses

Controlling expenses is vital to achieving a healthy bottom line. Monitoring and analyzing practice expenditures and consistently adhering to the budget throughout the year aids in accomplishing this function. Strategic agreements with suppliers and the application of accounting and financial controls can also keep expenses in check.

◼ Budgeting and Planning

Budgeting and planning is the third area of financial management. The manager must develop budgets that meet the practice's short-term cash needs. These plans also ensure that capital will be available when the practice wants to expand or purchase equipment. The manager must base planning documents and budgets on reasonable assumptions, yet make them flexible enough to be quickly adapted to changes in the external business environment or the practice's internal needs.

◼ Tax and Regulatory Agency Compliance

The fourth area of financial management is compliance with tax and regulatory agencies. Controls and documentation ensure that internal operations meet statutory requirements and, most importantly, that tax liabilities are paid on time. Financial management in a medical practice could easily be – and many times is – a full-time job. Many managers with financial responsibilities do not have an in-depth background in finance. Rather, they have transitioned to their positions from other roles.[1] Their challenge is to obtain the breadth of knowledge required to manage the finances of a business enterprise that generates millions of dollars in new charges each month while operating in a highly regulated, and increasingly litigious, environment; in other words, a medical practice.

Whether you are an early careerist or a seasoned medical practice professional, this volume will put you on the path to becoming and remaining an effective financial manager for your practice.

Body of Knowledge Review Series Contributors

Geraldine Amori, PhD, ARM, CPHRM
Douglas G. Anderson, FACMPE
James A. Barnes, MBA
Fred Beck, JD
Jerry D. Callahan Jr., CPA
Anthony J. DiPiazza, CPA
David N. Gans, MSHA, FACMPE
Robert L. Garrie, MPA, RHIA
Edward Gulko, MBA, FACMPE, FACHE, LNHA
Kenneth T. Hertz, CMPE
Steven M. Hudson, CFP, CFS, CRPC
Jerry Lagle, MBA, CPA, FACMPE
Michael Landers
Gary Lewins, FACMPE, CPA, FHFMA
Ken Mace, MA, CMPE
Jeffrey Milburn, MBA, CMPE
Michael A. O'Connell, MHA, FACMPE, CHE
Dawn M. Oetjen, PhD, MHA
Reid M. Oetjen, PhD, MSHSA
Pamela E. Paustian, MSM, RHIA
David Peterson, MBA, FACMPE
Lisa H. Schneck, MSJ
Frederic R. Simmons Jr., CPA
Thomas E. Sisson, CPA
Donna J. Slovensky, PhD, RHIA, FAHIMA
Jerry M. Trimm, PhD, FHIMSS
Stephen L. Wagner, PhD, FACMPE
Lee Ann H. Webster, MA, CPA, FACMPE
Susan Wendling-Aloi, MPA, FACMPE
Warren C. White Jr., FACMPE
Lawrence Wolper, MBA, FACMPE, CMC
Lorraine C. Woods, FACMPE
James R. Wurts, FACMPE

Learning Objectives

AFTER READING THIS VOLUME, the medical practice executive will be able to accomplish the following tasks:

- Develop and implement the organization's budget to achieve organizational objectives;

- Establish internal controls for cash management and external audits;

- Develop and implement revenue cycle management and accounts receivable management;

- Analyze and monitor financial performance and report financial results to stakeholders;

- Establish and maintain the organization's banking, investment, and other financial relationships; and

- Develop relationships with individual insurance carriers to optimize contract negotiations and maintenance of existing contracts.

First Spin in the Revenue Cycle: Good Front-End Practices Make the Difference[2]

LIKE OTHER INDUSTRIES, health care today tries to do more with less. Physician practices – like hospitals and other medical organizations – operate "lean," using a minimum of people to get the work done. This approach is boosted by a newfound focus on "best practices": heightening efficiency to maximize time and effort.

However, sometimes the front end of physician offices operates so lean that it compromises the quality of information captured. Office staff cannot commit the time to ensure thorough patient registration, referral management, and health coverage verification. As a result, the revenue cycle suffers. Payers reject billed claims that lack accurate demographic and insurance information. Poor front-end practices produce poor billing statements that can drastically decrease the incoming flow of cash.

Problems with Registration

Patient registration performed in a practice's front office is often inadequate to meet the needs of back-office billing staff. In this "do more with less" world, too few front-desk employees must often strive to perform too many tasks, such as:

- Greeting patients;
- Collecting demographic and insurance information;
- Booking appointments;
- Coordinating the referral process;
- Answering phones; and
- Managing the office's patient flow.

Practices often add the registration process to an already full plate. Such a burden may result in less attention to the registration process and its quality. As a result, back-office staff faces claims cleanup to rectify missing data required by third-party payers.

Create a Central Registration Unit

Registration generates an organization's bread and butter with respect to timely reimbursement. Administrators should consider it a priority to streamline the process and keep it cost-effective. A central registration unit is one solution to streamline the registration process. By designating key staff members as registration experts, a practice can shift the process from the front desk to employees who have dedicated responsibility for it. This frees front-desk staff to manage patient flow and appointments.

Although a group may need to invest time and training for a central registration unit, the return from increased cash flow should offset upfront expenditures. When operational design permits, a practice might reorganize existing staff into the registration unit rather than hire additional employees.

Separate Registration from the Front Desk

Another option is to separate the registration process from the front-desk setting. A full-time registration clerk in the back office can work

Knowledge Needs

FINANCIAL MANAGEMENT REQUIRES a diverse set of skills and knowledge to successfully ensure sufficient resources for operations, capital acquisitions, and retirement needs. The practice executive needs to:

- Understand both accounting and finance, including:
  - Double-entry accounting,
  - Generally accepted accounting principles,
  - Tax and regulatory reporting requirements,
  - Cash flow analysis,
  - Analysis of potential capital expenditures,
  - Investment risk and returns,
  - Financial planning,
  - Accounts payable, and
  - Accounts receivable;
- Possess the ability to identify financial partners to help navigate through the financial world;
- Understand various software programs and applications, such as practice management systems, electronic health records, accounting packages, and spreadsheet programs;

- Acquire a basic understanding of the myriad reimbursement systems:
  - Medicare/Medicaid,
  - Fee for service,
  - Case rates, and
  - Capitation;
- Negotiate contracts with third-party payers;
- Understand billing systems; and
- Discuss and fairly adjust compensation and benefit levels.

Of the tasks that compose the *Medical Practice Management Body of Knowledge* Financial Management domain, the one most integral to reimbursement is understanding third-party payers and how to negotiate profitable contracts for each of the practice's services. This task requires knowledge that falls outside of the field of finance. Many would consider negotiation skills a subset of communication skills. The reasons they are mentioned herein is because the manager must understand the legal implications of agreeing to and signing contracts – and then following through by properly managing each contract. This calls for knowledge in the legal field as well as knowledge about human resource management and facilitation.

Perhaps the most important skill a financial manager needs is the ability to communicate. Identifying financial issues and performing analyses are important, but this knowledge is of little use if it stays on spreadsheets. The medical practice administrator's main task is to inform the practice's physician leaders of financial results and the causes that produced those results. Then the administrator must use well-honed presentation skills to effectively explain options to physician leaders and guide them to make decisions that will produce measurable improvements in the practice's future – and ultimately, the executive's career.

Chapter 1 **Managing a Budget to Achieve Organizational Objectives**

I don't have too much time for fiction.

— RONALD REAGAN,
40TH U.S. PRESIDENT
*(Memoirs of former budget director
David A. Stockman)*

BUDGETING IS AN ACCOUNTING AND PLANNING TOOL that practices can use to plan for the future. Unfortunately, finding an excuse to not prepare a budget is easy, especially with all the other responsibilities that administrators face. One rationale holds that budgets are for large practices only and are too complicated to benefit smaller practices.

The truth is that budgets can benefit almost every practice. By taking the time to prepare a simple budget, a practice can anticipate potential problems, such as cash shortages, and prepare for them. Practice leaders can identify potential opportunities and plan to capitalize on them. A budget provides a framework for monitoring and evaluating operational and accounting performance. Approved budgets improve organizational efficiency by authorizing expenditures of practice resources, thus avoiding multiple requests for approval of these items. Finally, an effective budget process facilitates communication within the practice because it involves key people in different departments and functions across the practice.

Budgeting vs. Financial Accounting

Although budgets depend on financial accounting systems, they are different in some important ways. While the accounting system reports transactions that happened in the past, a budget anticipates transactions that will happen in the future. Financial statements focus on external reporting and must be presented in a format prescribed by generally accepted accounting principles (GAAP) or some other comprehensive basis of accounting, such as the cash or tax basis. Conversely, because budgets focus on the internal needs of management, administrators may tailor the format of budgets to fit the needs of the organization.

The Budget's Relationship to Strategic and Operational Planning

Strategic planning is the development of a long-range course of action (five to ten years) to achieve the medical group's goals. Operational planning is the development of short-term plans to achieve goals identified in the strategic plan. Operational plans cover periods ranging from one week or a month to several years. Budgeting is the financial portion of the operational plan; it defines the resources available to attain the practice's short-term and long-term goals.

To obtain the most benefit from the budget process, a practice should first have a strategic plan and establish its goals for the budget period. In some cases, the administrator may need to begin the budget process as a basis for stimulating discussion to assist the board in establishing its objectives.

◢ The Budget Process

Many people consider budgets to be an activity that an administrator or finance department carries out in isolation, without consulting the rest of the practice. This assumption is far from true. Although the administrator or a key financial person usually has overall responsibility for preparing and coordinating the budget, the process is most beneficial when key clinical and administrative personnel, physicians, and other members of the governing body participate in the process and refer to the organization's operational and strategic plans.

In smaller practices, the outside accountant may occasionally assist in this process. The role of an outside accountant in the budget process should be purely that of an advisor or facilitator; insiders should determine the organization's objectives and control its related budget process.

Obtain Data from Department Managers

The administrator (or other designated budget coordinator) reviews the practice's goals and objectives, determines what data are needed, and prepares the working documents necessary for obtaining this information. As a general rule, the administrator should delegate the task of gathering budget amounts to the lowest level appropriate, such as department managers for the cost and expense budgets and the patient accounting manager for revenue amounts. Because of the sensitive and confidential nature of physician compensation, the administrator or a key financial person normally prepares the provider compensation budget.

Assemble Budget/Revise as Necessary

After receiving requested data from key clinical and administrative personnel, the administrator assimilates it into budget form. The administrator identifies problem areas and inconsistencies with the numbers as compared to the practice's goals, and modifies the budget in coordination with the participants and governing body. The practice may need to revise its business plan if desired physician compensation or other objectives are incompatible with financial realities.

Board Approval

After assembling a budget that is consistent with the organization's goals and financial realities, the administrator presents it to the governing body for approval.

Ongoing Monitoring/Revisions

Throughout the budget period, the practice monitors the actual results vs. the budget projections and stays alert for changes in the operating environment that necessitate changes to the budget or operations.

To assist practice leadership in monitoring the budget, many accounting systems have report writing features, such as a comparison of income statement balances against the budget. Many client accounting software packages enable users to produce these types of statements, so practices that use an outside accountant to prepare financial statements can most likely request and receive these reports.

◢ Types of Budgets

Although the term *budget* implies a single process, a practice often needs several budgets to address its specific needs. The practice's mission, structure, and approach to management determines the different types of budgets it needs to fulfill its strategic and operational plans. The exhibits contained in this chapter show the various budgets used by a hypothetical practice, Deep South Obstetrics and Gynecology, P.C. This practice is purely fictitious; any resemblance to an existing practice is a coincidence.[3]

Revenue Budget (May Incorporate Separate Statistics Budget)

The revenue budget is the usual starting point for the budget process. Many of the amounts determined in other parts of the budget process depend on the revenue budget. Some practices prepare a separate statistics budget that forecasts provider production levels, while other practices incorporate this process into their revenue budget.

Statistics Budget

The advantage of having a separate statistics budget is that it provides uniform assumptions regarding volume of services, types of services, rate of inflation, and so forth, for all of the practice's budgets.

Accurate volume estimates are critical to the success of the entire budget process. Unfortunately, predicting volume is often difficult because the number and type of patients depend on many factors, some within the control of the practice and some outside of its control. Marketing campaigns, new managed care contracts, termination of managed care contracts, area business expansion, and demographic shifts in the community are only some of the activities that can affect practice volumes. If it overestimates volume, a practice might increase overhead expenses and therefore reduce the practice's net income. If a practice underestimates volume, it risks losing patients to competitors and incurring increased operating costs caused by staff overtime and inefficiencies resulting from overcrowding.

Revenue Budget

The revenue budget combines volume information from the statistics budget with projected reimbursement information. Practice personnel need to exercise care in determining revenue budget amounts. Changes in payer fee schedules, payer mix, Current Procedural Terminology coding rules, deductibles, and the practice's chargemaster can change the dollar amount of reimbursement, as well as the gross collection rate often used to compute budget revenues. Additional considerations are projected capitation income, ancillary revenue, and other sources of income.

Note that the revenue budget in Exhibit 1 takes into consideration overall volume growth, as well as volume generated by a new physician and other revenue. This sample budget revises the expected gross collection rate of the practice based on the anticipated

EXHIBIT 1
Revenue Budget

DEEP SOUTH OBSTETRICS AND GYNECOLOGY, P.C.
Revenue Budget – 2008

Description/Month		Jan	Feb	Mar	Apr	May	Jun
Charges 20X7		820,000	685,000	855,000	825,000	845,000	805,000
2008 growth	3%	24,600	20,550	25,650	24,750	25,350	24,150
New Doctor							
Charges 20X8		844,600	705,550	880,650	849,750	870,350	829,150
Projected collections rate							
−2007 charges 51.7%							
−2008 charges 52.5%							
Collections 2008		409,981	417,285	417,785	402,512	456,576	449,818

Payer	Collection Rate	Mix	Weighted Collection Rate
Medicare FFS	52%	23%	11.96%
Medicare HMO	47%	5%	2.35%
Commercial HMO	53%	34%	18.02%
Commercial PPO	57%	25%	14.25%
Commercial	60%	4%	2.40%
Medicaid	40%	6%	2.40%
Self Pay	37%	3%	1.11%
		100%	52.49%

OTHER REVENUE
Contract Ultrasounds

	Jan	Feb	Mar	Apr	May	Jun
Studies Per Month	100	90	105	95	105	100
Rate	200	200	200	200	200	200
Revenue	20,000	18,000	21,000	19,000	21,000	20,000
Other Revenue	3,750	3,750	3,750	3,750	3,750	3,750
Total Other Revenue	23,750	21,750	24,750	22,750	24,750	23,750

Jul	Aug	Sep	Oct	Nov	Dec	Total
755,000	780,000	810,000	860,000	800,000	780,000	9,620,000
22,650	23,400	24,300	25,800	24,000	23,400	288,600
	25,000	40,000	60,000	70,000	60,000	255,000
777,650	828,400	874,300	945,800	894,000	863,400	10,163,600
449,278	425,760	417,512	443,260	472,056	486,934	5,248,756

Jul	Aug	Sep	Oct	Nov	Dec	Total
95	95	105	105	100	90	1,185
200	200	200	200	200	200	
19,000	19,000	21,000	21,000	20,000	18,000	237,000
3,750	3,750	3,750	3,750	3,750	3,750	45,000
22,750	22,750	24,750	24,750	23,750	21,750	282,000

collection rates and payer mix. In addition to the amount of revenue available to the practice, the revenue budget needs to forecast when the revenue will be received. Depending on the nature of a practice, its basis of accounting, and its budgets, either the master budget or the cash budget will need to include these amounts.

Capital Budget

The capital budget plans for purchases of assets that have useful lives greater than one year. A medical practice may acquire some assets because they are necessary for patient care. For example, a cardiology practice might purchase an automatic external defibrillator, hoping that it would not need to be used, but it would be available if a patient experiences cardiac arrest.

A practice may acquire other assets because they offer a positive economic return to the practice. Use of discounted cash flow techniques helps determine whether a potential investment has an acceptable rate of return.

The cost of capital equipment or a building is depreciated, or spread over its useful life, according to rules promulgated by GAAP or the Internal Revenue Code. The related depreciation expense will be reflected in the practice's expense budget.

The sample capital budget for Deep South Obstetrics and Gynecology, P.C., is shown in Exhibit 2.

Expense Budget (May Incorporate Separate Staff Budget)

The expense budget establishes the anticipated expenses for the practice. It addresses each expense category in the practice, such as support staff salaries and fringe benefits, depreciation and amortization, supplies, occupancy expenses, and purchased services.

Because much of the expense data depends on production, this budget may only be prepared after completing the related revenue or statistics budget. In preparing the expense budget, the manager needs to consider cost behavior in relationship to volume. Variable costs, such as medical supplies, fluctuate directly with volume.

Fixed costs, such as rent, remain the same over a relevant range of activity.

Some practices prepare a separate staff budget because of the significance of medical practice staff salaries in relationship to total overhead. Exhibit 3 gives an example of a staff budget. Note that this budget includes projected salary and benefits increases, as well as the addition of staff members when a new physician joins the practice in August.

Exhibit 4 shows the expense budget for the hypothetical practice, Deep South Obstetrics and Gynecology, P.C. In anticipation of the new physician's arrival at the practice, this cash basis expense budget includes increased expenditures for medical supplies during July.

Provider Compensation Budget

The provider compensation budget forecasts the amount of profits available to pay physicians and other providers. For physician-owned practices, the amount by which practice revenue exceeds the related expenses generally limits the total amount of compensation and other distributions to the physician-owners. The method of distribution varies according to the type of entity and the practice's physician compensation formula.

Medical groups that are part of larger integrated delivery systems or are owned by a parent corporation may receive subsidies that can be used to offset operating costs or pay physicians. Accordingly, these organizations need to include both the amount of physician compensation and the amount of operating subsidy in their budgets.

Exhibit 5 shows the provider compensation budget for Deep South Obstetrics and Gynecology, P.C. Note that this budget incorporates anticipated bonuses as well as the addition of a physician in July.

EXHIBIT 2

Capital Budget

DEEP SOUTH OBSTETRICS AND GYNECOLOGY, P.C.
Capital Budget – 2008

Loc.	Description	Vendor	Computers	Off. Equip.
	Excess buildout			
	Satellite office furniture			
	Waiting	Office Inc		
	Nurses/MA Station	Office Inc		
	Front Desk	Office Inc		
	Medical Records	Office Inc		
	Ultrasound room	Office Inc		
	Exam Rooms(3)	PSS		
	Dictation room	Office Inc		
	Doctor's Office	Office Inc		
	Artwork	Art store		
	Other			
	Satellite office equipment			
	Computers/monitors(3)	Dell	3,000	
	Printers(3)	Dell	750	
	Routers/communication	Cisco	1,000	
	Phone system	Comdial		3,000
	Phones(7)	Comdial		1,500
	Ultrasound system	GE		
	Subtotal		4,750	4,500
	Sales tax		285	270
	Grand Total		5,035	4,770

Depreciation	Total	Monthly
Pre 2008 additions	$65,000	$5,417
2008 additions	25,000	4,167
Total	$90,000	$9,583

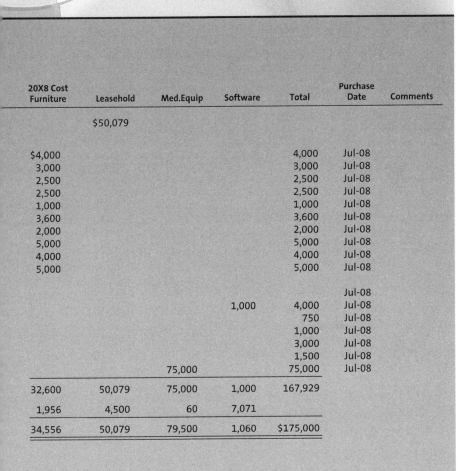

20X8 Cost Furniture	Leasehold	Med.Equip	Software	Total	Purchase Date	Comments
	$50,079					
$4,000				4,000	Jul-08	
3,000				3,000	Jul-08	
2,500				2,500	Jul-08	
2,500				2,500	Jul-08	
1,000				1,000	Jul-08	
3,600				3,600	Jul-08	
2,000				2,000	Jul-08	
5,000				5,000	Jul-08	
4,000				4,000	Jul-08	
5,000				5,000	Jul-08	
					Jul-08	
			1,000	4,000	Jul-08	
				750	Jul-08	
				1,000	Jul-08	
				3,000	Jul-08	
				1,500	Jul-08	
		75,000		75,000	Jul-08	
32,600	50,079	75,000	1,000	167,929		
1,956	4,500	60	7,071			
34,556	50,079	79,500	1,060	$175,000		

EXHIBIT 3

Staff Budget

DEEP SOUTH OBSTETRICS AND GYNECOLOGY, P.C.
Staff Budget – 2008

Pay periods per month					2	2	3
	FTE			Hourly			
Department/Position	1-Jan	1-Aug	Name	Rate	Jan	Feb	Mar
General administrative							
Administrator	1.00	1.00		$43.25	6,920	6,920	10,380
Administrator bonus							
Secretary	1.00	1.00		$12.02	1,923	1,923	2,885
Total general administrative	2.00	2.00			8,843	8,843	13,265
Patient accounting							
Patient accounting manager	1.00	1.00		$19.23	3,077	3,077	4,615
Patient accounting staff	1.00	1.00		$15.00	2,400	2,400	3,600
Patient accounting staff	1.00	1.00		$15.29	2,446	2,446	3,670
Patient accounting staff	1.00	1.00		$15.40	2,464	2,464	3,696
Patient accounting staff	1.00	1.00		$15.85	2,536	2,536	3,804
Total patient accounting	5.00	5.00			12,923	12,923	19,385
Front desk							
Medical receptionists Super	1.00	1.00		$16.35	2,616	2,616	3,924
Medical receptionists	1.00	1.00		$12.40	1,984	1,984	2,976
Medical receptionists	1.00	1.00		$12.75	2,040	2,040	3,060
Medical receptionists	1.00	1.00		$13.00	2,080	2,080	3,120
Medical receptionists	1.00	1.00		$12.75	2,040	2,040	3,060
Medical receptionists	1.00	1.00		$13.50	2,160	2,160	3,240
Medical receptionists	1.00	1.00		$13.48	2,157	2,157	3,235
Medical receptionists		1.00		$13.25			
Total front desk	7.00	8.00			15,077	15,077	22,615
Transcription							
Transcriptionists.	1.00	1.00		$13.46	2,154	2,154	3,230
Transcriptionists.	1.00	1.00		$13.46	2,154	2,154	3,230
Total transcription	2.00	2.00			4,307	4,307	6,461
Medical records							
Medical records supervisor	1.00	1.00		$14.75	2,360	2,360	3,540
Medical records clerk	1.00	1.00		$11.00	1,760	1,760	2,640
Medical records clerk	1.00	1.00		$10.31	1,650	1,650	2,474
Medical records clerk		1.00		$10.50			
Total medical records	3.00	4.00			5,770	5,770	8,654

| 2 | 2 | 2 | 2 | 2 | 3 | 2 | 2 | 2 | |
Apr	May	Jun	Jul	Aug	Sep	Oct	Nov	Dec	Total
6,920	6,920	6,920	7,197	7,197	10,795	7,197	7,197	7,197	91,759
								10,000	10,000
1,923	1,923	1,923	2,000	2,000	3,000	2,000	2,000	2,000	25,502
8,843	8,843	8,843	9,197	9,197	13,795	9,197	9,197	19,197	127,261
3,077	3,077	3,077	3,200	3,200	4,800	3,200	3,200	3,200	40,798
2,400	2,400	2,400	2,496	2,496	3,744	2,496	2,496	2,496	31,824
2,446	2,446	2,446	2,544	2,544	3,816	2,544	2,544	2,544	32,439
2,464	2,464	2,464	2,563	2,563	3,844	2,563	2,563	2,563	32,673
2,536	2,536	2,536	2,637	2,637	3,956	2,637	2,637	2,637	33,627
12,923	12,923	12,923	13,440	13,440	20,160	13,440	13,440	13,440	171,362
2,616	2,616	2,616	2,721	2,721	4,081	2,721	2,721	2,721	34,688
1,984	1,984	1,984	2,063	2,063	3,095	2,063	2,063	2,063	26,308
2,040	2,040	2,040	2,122	2,122	3,182	2,122	2,122	2,122	27,050
2,080	2,080	2,080	2,163	2,163	3,245	2,163	2,163	2,163	27,581
2,040	2,040	2,040	2,122	2,122	3,182	2,122	2,122	2,122	27,050
2,160	2,160	2,160	2,246	2,246	3,370	2,246	2,246	2,246	28,642
2,157	2,157	2,157	2,243	2,243	3,365	2,243	2,243	2,243	28,599
				2,205	3,307	2,205	2,205	2,205	12,126
15,077	15,077	15,077	15,680	17,885	26,827	17,885	17,885	17,885	212,045
2,154	2,154	2,154	2,240	2,240	3,360	2,240	2,240	2,240	28,557
2,154	2,154	2,154	2,240	2,240	3,360	2,240	2,240	2,240	28,557
4,307	4,307	4,307	4,479	4,479	6,719	4,479	4,479	4,479	57,113
2,360	2,360	2,360	2,454	2,454	3,682	2,454	2,454	2,454	31,294
1,760	1,760	1,760	1,830	1,830	2,746	1,830	1,830	1,830	23,338
1,650	1,650	1,650	1,716	1,716	2,573	1,716	1,716	1,716	21,874
				1,747	2,621	1,747	1,747	1,747	9,610
5,770	5,770	5,770	6,000	7,748	11,621	7,748	7,748	7,748	86,114

EXHIBIT 3 *(continued)*

Staff Budget

Pay periods per month					2	2	3
Department/Position	FTE 1-Jan	1-Aug	Name	Hourly Rate	Jan	Feb	Mar
Nursing							
Registered nurse	1.00	1.00		$23.00	3,680	3,680	5,520
Registered nurse	1.00	1.00		$23.76	3,802	3,802	5,702
Registered nurse	1.00	1.00		$22.50	3,600	3,600	5,400
Registered nurse	1.00	1.00		$23.05	3,688	3,688	5,532
Registered nurse		1.00		$23.00			
Licensed practical nurse	1.00	1.00		$16.39	2,622	2,622	3,934
Licensed practical nurse	1.00	1.00		$16.30	2,608	2,608	3,912
Medical assistant	1.00	1.00		$13.00	2,080	2,080	3,120
Medical assistant	1.00	1.00		$12.18	1,949	1,949	2,923
Medical assistant	1.00	1.00		$12.75	2,040	2,040	3,060
Medical assistant	1.00	1.00		$13.50	2,160	2,160	3,240
Medical assistant	1.00	1.00		$13.20	2,112	2,112	3,168
Medical assistant	1.00	1.00		$13.25	2,120	2,120	3,180
Medical assistant		1.00		$13.25			
Total nursing	12.00	14.00			32,461	32,461	48,691
Lab							
Lab tech	1.00	1.00		$12.50	2,000	2,000	3,000
Lab tech part time	0.50	0.50		$12.50	1,000	1,000	1,500
Total lab	1.50	1.50			3,000	3,000	4,500
Ultrasound							
Ultrasound Tech supervisor	1.00	1.00		$28.00	4,480	4,480	6,720
Ultrasound Tech	1.00	1.00		$22.44	3,590	3,590	5,386
Ultrasound Tech	1.00	1.00		$22.00	3,520	3,520	5,280
Ultrasound Tech part time	0.50	0.50		$23.40	1,872	1,872	2,808
	3.50	3.50			13,462	13,462	20,194
	36.00	40.00			95,843	95,843	143,765
Payroll Taxes					7,667	7,667	11,501
Employee Benefits							
2007 Monthly benefits costs				16,250	16,250	16,250	16,250
2008 Budgeted increase				7%	1,138	1,138	1,138
2008 Budgeted benefits costs					17,388	17,388	17,388

Budgeted increase eff. July 1   0.04

Add new doctor 7/15/X8

Add satellite office 8/1/X8 with 1.00 FTE receptionist, medical records clerk, registered nurse and medical assistant

| 2 | 2 | 2 | 2 | 2 | 3 | 2 | 2 | 2 | |
Apr	May	Jun	Jul	Aug	Sep	Oct	Nov	Dec	Total
3,680	3,680	3,680	3,827	3,827	5,741	3,827	3,827	3,827	48,797
3,802	3,802	3,802	3,954	3,954	5,930	3,954	3,954	3,954	50,409
3,600	3,600	3,600	3,744	3,744	5,616	3,744	3,744	3,744	47,736
3,688	3,688	3,688	3,836	3,836	5,753	3,836	3,836	3,836	48,903
				3,827	5,741	3,827	3,827	3,827	21,050
2,622	2,622	2,622	2,727	2,727	4,091	2,727	2,727	2,727	34,773
2,608	2,608	2,608	2,712	2,712	4,068	2,712	2,712	2,712	34,582
2,080	2,080	2,080	2,163	2,163	3,245	2,163	2,163	2,163	27,581
1,949	1,949	1,949	2,027	2,027	3,040	2,027	2,027	2,027	25,841
2,040	2,040	2,040	2,122	2,122	3,182	2,122	2,122	2,122	27,050
2,160	2,160	2,160	2,246	2,246	3,370	2,246	2,246	2,246	28,642
2,112	2,112	2,112	2,196	2,196	3,295	2,196	2,196	2,196	28,005
2,120	2,120	2,120	2,205	2,205	3,307	2,205	2,205	2,205	28,111
				2,205	3,307	2,205	2,205	2,205	12,126
32,461	32,461	32,461	33,759	39,791	59,687	39,791	39,791	39,791	463,606
2,000	2,000	2,000	2,080	2,080	3,120	2,080	2,080	2,080	26,520
1,000	1,000	1,000	2,080	2,080	3,120	2,080	2,080	2,080	20,020
3,000	3,000	3,000	4,160	4,160	6,240	4,160	4,160	4,160	46,540
4,480	4,480	4,480	4,659	4,659	6,989	4,659	4,659	4,659	59,405
3,590	3,590	3,590	3,734	3,734	5,601	3,734	3,734	3,734	47,609
3,520	3,520	3,520	3,661	3,661	5,491	3,661	3,661	3,661	46,675
1,872	1,872	1,872	3,894	3,894	5,841	3,894	3,894	3,894	37,477
13,462	13,462	13,462	15,948	15,948	23,922	15,948	15,948	15,948	191,166
95,843	95,843	95,843	102,664	112,648	168,972	112,648	112,648	122,648	1,355,208
7,667	7,667	7,667	8,213	9,012	13,518	9,012	9,012	9,812	108,417
16,250	16,250	16,250	18,055	18,055	18,055	18,055	18,055	18,055	205,830
1,138	1,138	1,138	1,264	1,264	1,264	1,264	1,264	1,264	14,408
17,388	17,388	17,388	19,319	19,319	19,319	19,319	19,319	19,319	220,238

EXHIBIT 4

Expense Budget

DEEP SOUTH OBSTETRICS AND GYNECOLOGY, P.C.
Expense Budget – 2008

	Jan	Feb	Mar	Apr	May	Jun
Services and General Expenses						
Malpractice insurance	$80,000			$80,000		
Medical and surgical supplies	15,000	15,000	15,000	15,000	15,000	15,000
Depreciation	5,417	5,417	5,417	5,417	5,417	5,417
Amortization	417	417	417	417	417	417
Rent	27,500	27,500	27,500	27,500	27,500	27,500
Information technology	7,500	7,500	7,500	7,500	7,500	7,500
Other general and administrative exp.	13,500	13,500	13,500	13,500	13,500	13,500
Total services and general expenses	$149,334	$69,334	$69,334	$149,334	$69,334	$69,334

Master Budget

The master budget brings together the practice's various budgets in either formal or informal financial statement formats. The master budget in Exhibit 6 gives the income statement amounts from the various budgets by month. The master budget in Exhibit 7 shows the annual budget amounts compared to the prior year actual, computes the variance, indicates the source budget, and provides an explanation of significant changes.

Cash Budget

The cash budget is the cornerstone for short-term cash management in a practice. It provides management with a forecast of the organization's short-term availability of cash, its need for supplemental cash in the form of a loan or line of credit to meet predicted

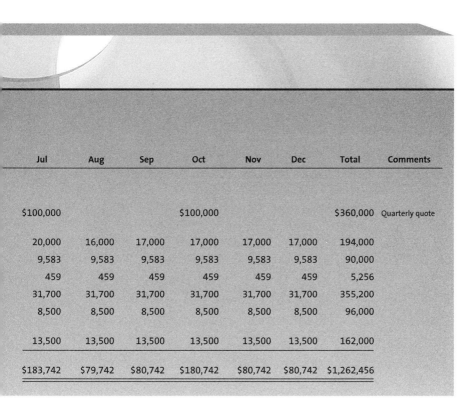

Jul	Aug	Sep	Oct	Nov	Dec	Total	Comments
$100,000			$100,000			$360,000	Quarterly quote
20,000	16,000	17,000	17,000	17,000	17,000	194,000	
9,583	9,583	9,583	9,583	9,583	9,583	90,000	
459	459	459	459	459	459	5,256	
31,700	31,700	31,700	31,700	31,700	31,700	355,200	
8,500	8,500	8,500	8,500	8,500	8,500	96,000	
13,500	13,500	13,500	13,500	13,500	13,500	162,000	
$183,742	$79,742	$80,742	$180,742	$80,742	$80,742	$1,262,456	

expenses, and any periods with excess cash available for short-term investments.

Exhibit 8 shows the monthly cash budget for the hypothetical practice, Deep South Obstetrics and Gynecology, P.C. Because this practice is a cash basis practice, its cash budget requires only a few adjustments to translate net income per the operating budget to projected cash flow. Accrual basis practices usually have more differences between operating net income and cash flow. An alternate approach is the direct method, which itemizes cash receipts and disbursements rather than reconciling them to net income.

Departmental Budget

Larger practices or those with multiple locations, service lines, and/or specialties often prepare separate budgets for each department.

EXHIBIT 5
Provider Compensation Budget

DEEP SOUTH OBSTETRICS AND GYNECOLOGY, P.C.
Provider Compensation Budget – 2008

Physician/Extender	Jan	Feb	Mar	Apr	May	Jun
Base Salary						
Smith	15,000	15,000	15,000	15,000	15,000	15,000
Jones	15,000	15,000	15,000	15,000	15,000	15,000
Harris	16,667	16,667	16,667	16,667	16,667	16,667
Thruman	16,667	16,667	16,667	16,667	16,667	16,667
Dunn	16,667	16,667	16,667	16,667	16,667	16,667
Thompson	16,667	16,667	16,667	16,667	16,667	16,667
Cohen	16,667	16,667	16,667	16,667	16,667	16,667
New Doctor						
Total physicians	113,335	113,335	113,335	113,335	113,335	113,335
Bonuses						200,000
Grand total physicians	113,335	113,335	113,335	113,335	113,335	313,335
Physician payroll tax %	7.6%	7.6%	7.6%	7.6%	6.0%	1.4%
Physician payroll tax $	8,613	8,613	8,613	8,613	6,800	4,387
Physician benefits	34,000	34,000	34,000	34,000	34,000	34,000
Physician extenders						
Base Salary						
Bence	4,792	4,792	4,792	4,792	4,792	4,792
Davis	4,792	4,792	4,792	4,792	4,792	4,792
Starr	5,000	5,000	5,000	5,000	5,000	5,000
Total	14,584	14,584	14,584	14,584	14,584	14,584
Bonuses						10,000
Grand Total Extenders	14,584	14,584	14,584	14,584	14,584	24,584
Extenders payroll tax %	8.0%	8.0%	8.0%	8.0%	8.0%	8.0%
Extenders payroll tax $	1,167	1,167	1,167	1,167	1,167	1,967
Extenders benefits	3,000	3,000	3,000	3,000	3,000	3,000

Jul	Aug	Sep	Oct	Nov	Dec	Total
15,000	15,000	15,000	15,000	15,000	15,000	180,000
15,000	15,000	15,000	15,000	15,000	15,000	180,000
16,667	16,667	16,667	16,667	16,667	16,667	200,004
16,667	16,667	16,667	16,667	16,667	16,667	200,004
16,667	16,667	16,667	16,667	16,667	16,667	200,004
16,667	16,667	16,667	16,667	16,667	16,667	200,004
16,667	16,667	16,667	16,667	16,667	16,667	200,004
12,500	12,500	12,500	12,500	12,500	12,500	75,000
125,835	125,835	125,835	125,835	125,835	125,835	1,435,020
					200,000	400,000
125,835	125,835	125,835	125,835	125,835	325,835	1,835,020
2.0%	2.0%	2.0%	2.0%	2.0%	2.0%	
2,517	2,517	2,517	2,517	2,517	6,517	64,741
37,000	37,000	37,000	37,000	37,000	37,000	426,000
4,792	4,792	4,792	4,792	4,792	4,792	57,504
4,792	4,792	4,792	4,792	4,792	4,792	57,504
5,000	5,000	5,000	5,000	5,000	5,000	60,000
14,584	14,584	14,584	14,584	14,584	14,584	175,008
					15,000	25,000
14,584	14,584	14,584	14,584	14,584	29,584	200,008
8.0%	8.0%	8.0%	8.0%	8.0%	8.0%	
1,167	1,167	1,167	1,167	1,167	2,367	16,001
3,000	3,000	3,000	3,000	3,000	3,000	36,000

EXHIBIT 6

Master Budget by Month

DEEP SOUTH OBSTETRICS AND GYNECOLOGY, P.C.
Master Budget by Month – 2008

	Jan	Feb	Mar	Apr	May
Charges	844,600	705,550	880,650	849,750	870,350
Revenues:					
Net fee-for-service revenue	409,981	417,285	417,785	402,512	456,576
Capitation revenue					
Other	23,750	21,750	24,750	22,750	24,750
Net revenue	433,731	439,035	442,535	425,262	481,326
Operating Expenses					
Salaries and benefits					
Staff salaries	95,843	95,843	143,765	95,843	95,843
Payroll taxes	7,667	7,667	11,501	7,667	7,667
Employee Benefits	17,388	17,388	17,388	17,388	17,388
Total salaries and benefits	120,898	120,898	172,653	120,898	120,898
Services and General Expenses					
Malpractice insurance	80,000	–	–	80,000	–
Medical and surgical supplies	15,000	15,000	15,000	15,000	15,000
Depreciation	5,417	5,417	5,417	5,417	5,417
Amortization	417	417	417	417	417
Rent	27,500	27,500	27,500	27,500	27,500
Information technology	7,500	7,500	7,500	7,500	7,500
Other general and administrative exp.	13,500	13,500	13,500	13,500	13,500
Total services and general expenses	149,334	69,334	69,334	149,334	69,334
Provider-related expenses					
Physician salaries	113,335	113,335	113,335	113,335	113,335
Physician payroll taxes	8,613	8,613	8,613	8,613	6,800
Physician benefits	34,000	34,000	34,000	34,000	34,000
Total physician costs	155,948	155,948	155,948	155,948	154,135
Nurse practitioner salaries	14,584	14,584	14,584	14,584	14,584
Nurse practitioner payroll taxes	1,167	1,167	1,167	1,167	1,167
Nurse practitioner benefits	3,000	3,000	3,000	3,000	3,000
Total nurse practitioner costs	18,751	18,751	18,751	18,751	18,751
Total provider costs	174,699	174,699	174,699	174,699	172,886
Total Operating Expenses	444,931	364,931	416,687	444,931	363,118
Income from Operations	(11,200)	74,103	25,848	(19,670)	118,208
Nonmedical costs					
Interest and taxes	750	750	750	750	750
Income (Loss)	(11,950)	73,353	25,098	(20,420)	117,458

Jun	Jul	Aug	Sep	Oct	Nov	Dec	Total
829,150	777,650	828,400	874,300	945,800	894,000	863,400	10,163,600
449,818	449,278	425,760	417,512	443,260	472,056	486,934	5,248,756
23,750	22,750	22,750	24,750	24,750	23,750	21,750	282,000
473,568	472,028	448,510	442,262	468,010	495,806	508,684	5,530,756
95,843	102,664	112,648	168,972	112,648	112,648	122,648	1,355,208
7,667	8,213	9,012	13,518	9,012	9,012	9,812	108,417
17,388	19,319	19,319	19,319	19,319	19,319	19,319	220,238
120,898	130,196	140,978	201,808	140,978	140,978	151,778	1,683,862
–	100,000	–	–	100,000	–	–	360,000
15,000	20,000	16,000	17,000	17,000	17,000	17,000	194,000
5,417	9,583	9,583	9,583	9,583	9,583	9,583	90,000
417	459	459	459	459	459	459	5,256
27,500	31,700	31,700	31,700	31,700	31,700	31,700	355,200
7,500	8,500	8,500	8,500	8,500	8,500	8,500	96,000
13,500	13,500	13,500	13,500	13,500	13,500	13,500	162,000
69,334	183,742	79,742	80,742	180,742	80,742	80,742	1,262,456
313,335	125,835	125,835	125,835	125,835	125,835	325,835	1,835,020
4,387	2,517	2,517	2,517	2,517	2,517	6,517	64,741
34,000	37,000	37,000	37,000	37,000	37,000	37,000	426,000
351,722	165,352	165,352	165,352	165,352	165,352	369,352	2,325,761
24,584	14,584	14,584	14,584	14,584	14,584	29,584	200,008
1,967	1,167	1,167	1,167	1,167	1,167	2,367	16,001
3,000	3,000	3,000	3,000	3,000	3,000	3,000	36,000
29,551	18,751	18,751	18,751	18,751	18,751	34,951	252,009
381,272	184,102	184,102	184,102	184,102	184,102	404,302	2,577,769
571,505	498,040	404,823	466,653	505,823	405,823	636,823	5,524,088
(97,936)	(26,013)	43,687	(24,391)	(37,813)	89,983	(128,139)	6,668
750	750	750	750	750	750	750	9,000
(98,686)	(26,763)	42,937	(25,141)	(38,563)	89,233	(128,889)	(2,332)

EXHIBIT 7

Master Budget by Year

DEEP SOUTH OBSTETRICS AND GYNECOLOGY, P.C.
Master Budget – 2008

	Source	Actual 2007
Charges	Revenue Budget	$9,620,000
Revenues:		
Net fee-for-service revenue	Revenue Budget	$4,980,000
Capitation revenue	Revenue Budget	
Other	Revenue Budget	270,000
Net revenue		5,250,000
Operating Expenses		
Salaries and benefits		
Staff salaries	Staff Budget	1,246,000
Payroll taxes	Staff Budget	100,000
Employee Benefits	Staff Budget	195,000
Total salaries and benefits		1,541,000
Services and General Expenses		
Malpractice insurance	Expense Budget	310,000
Medical and surgical supplies	Expense Budget	173,000
Depreciation	Expense Budget	75,000
Amortization	Expense Budget	5,000
Rent	Expense Budget	330,000
Information technology	Expense Budget	90,000
Other general and administrative exp.	Expense Budget	157,000
Total services and general expenses		1,140,000
Provider-related expenses		
Physician salaries	Provider Comp. Budget	1,865,000
Physician payroll taxes	Provider Comp. Budget	60,000
Physician benefits	Provider Comp. Budget	390,000
Total physician costs	Provider Comp. Budget	2,315,000
Nurse practitioner salaries	Provider Comp. Budget	196,000
Nurse practitioner payroll taxes	Provider Comp. Budget	15,600
Nurse practitioner benefits	Provider Comp. Budget	33,400
Total nurse practitioner costs	Provider Comp. Budget	245,000
Total provider costs	Provider Comp. Budget	2,560,000
Total Operating Expenses		5,241,000
Income from Operations		9,000
Nonmedical costs		
Interest and taxes		(10,000)
Income (Loss)		$(1,000)

Budget 2008	Variance $	%	
$10,163,600	$543,600	5.7%	Growth and new Dr. 7/08
5,248,756	268,756	5.4%	Growth and new Dr. 7/08
282,000	12,000	4.4%	Growth of contract ultrasounds
5,530,756	280,756	5.3%	
1,355,208	109,208	8.8%	New staff for new office 8/08
108,417	8,417	8.4%	New staff for new office 8/09
220,238	25,238	12.9%	New staff and higher health costs
1,683,862	142,862	9.3%	
360,000	50,000	16.1%	Malpractice increases per quote and new Doctor
194,000	21,000	12.1%	New office and more contract ultrasounds
90,000	15,000	20.0%	New office
5,256	256	5.1%	
355,200	25,200	7.6%	New office
96,000	6,000	6.7%	New office
162,000	5,000	3.2%	
1,262,456	122,456	10.7%	
1,835,020	(29,980)	−1.6%	Lower bonuses lower to fund new Dr. start-up
64,741	4,741	7.9%	New doctor
426,000	36,000	9.2%	New doctor and health increases
2,325,761	10,761	0.5%	
200,008	4,008	2.0%	Annual increases
16,001	401	2.6%	Annual increases
36,000	2,600	7.8%	Health increases
252,009	7,009	2.9%	
2,577,769	17,769	0.7%	
5,524,088	283,088	5.4%	
6,668	(2,332)	−25.9%	
(9,000)	1,000	−10.0%	
$(2,332)	$(1,332)	133.2%	

EXHIBIT 8

Cash Budget

DEEP SOUTH OBSTETRICS AND GYNECOLOGY, P.C.
Cash Budget – 2008

	Jan	Feb	Mar	Apr	May
Net Income(loss)	$(11,950)	$73,353	$25,098	$(20,420)	$117,458
Add back					
Depreciation	5,417	5,417	5,417	5,417	5,417
Amortization	417	417	417	417	417
Retirement accrual	25,000	25,000	25,000	25,000	25,000
LT Debt proceeds					
Total Adds	30,834	30,834	30,834	30,834	30,834
Subtract					
Principal payments	(2,000)	(1,950)	(1,900)	(1,850)	(1,800)
Retirement contribution			(300,000)		
Equipment purchases					
Total Subtracts	(2,000)	(1,950)	(301,900)	(1,850)	(1,800)
Cash flow for month	16,884	102,237	(245,968)	8,564	146,492
Cash, beginning of month	110,000	126,884	229,121	(16,847)	(8,282)
Cash, end of month	$126,884	$229,121	$(16,847)	$(8,282)	$138,210

These departmental budgets are then combined to form the organization's master budget.

Budget Methodologies

Fixed vs. Flexible

A fixed budget computes one best estimate for revenues and related expenses. Budget variances are based on differences between actual performance and the estimated set of numbers.

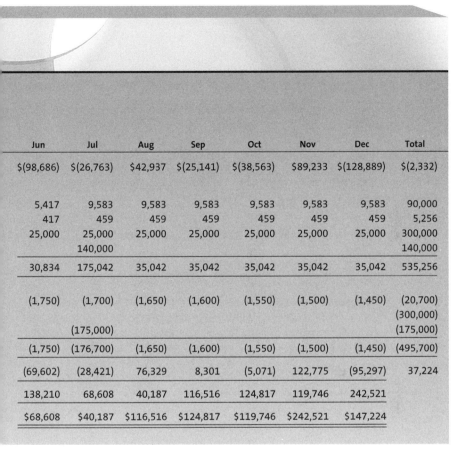

Jun	Jul	Aug	Sep	Oct	Nov	Dec	Total
$(98,686)	$(26,763)	$42,937	$(25,141)	$(38,563)	$89,233	$(128,889)	$(2,332)
5,417	9,583	9,583	9,583	9,583	9,583	9,583	90,000
417	459	459	459	459	459	459	5,256
25,000	25,000	25,000	25,000	25,000	25,000	25,000	300,000
	140,000						140,000
30,834	175,042	35,042	35,042	35,042	35,042	35,042	535,256
(1,750)	(1,700)	(1,650)	(1,600)	(1,550)	(1,500)	(1,450)	(20,700)
							(300,000)
	(175,000)						(175,000)
(1,750)	(176,700)	(1,650)	(1,600)	(1,550)	(1,500)	(1,450)	(495,700)
(69,602)	(28,421)	76,329	8,301	(5,071)	122,775	(95,297)	37,224
138,210	68,608	40,187	116,516	124,817	119,746	242,521	
$68,608	$40,187	$116,516	$124,817	$119,746	$242,521	$147,224	

A flexible budget assumes that actual results may vary and provides a mechanism for computing budget variances at different volume levels, based on a careful assessment of fixed, step-fixed, and variable costs. The advantage of a flexible budget is its ability to better assess financial performance at different activity levels. The primary disadvantage is that it is more time-consuming.

Traditional vs. Zero-Based

The traditional budget process uses prior and current year activity levels, revenues, and expenses as a basis for determining prospective values for the coming year. Conversely, zero-based budgeting begins each budget without considering past performance. Essentially, the budget starts at zero and all budget assumptions are reassessed.

The primary disadvantage of zero-based budgeting is that it is more time-consuming than traditional budgeting. The major advantage is that, because the zero-based budget process forces a practice to start over, it provides more insights into practice revenues and expenses. Thus, the practice will be more likely to set up its business in such a manner that by meeting its budget objectives it will also be successful in achieving its strategic or business plan.

◼ The Quest for Good Numbers

To get the most benefit from the budget process, a practice needs to ensure that it obtains accurate and well-supported numbers. Remember, the budget is the cornerstone of the practice's operational and strategic plans; good planning demands good numbers.

Common Budget Pitfalls

Practices sometimes sabotage a budget's potential effectiveness by using numbers that are too easy or too difficult to obtain, or by trying to complete the budget process in too short a time frame.

Failure to Allow Enough Time

Practice leaders should begin the budget process early enough to allow sufficient time to get good numbers. This can involve time to rework the initial numbers if they are inconsistent with each other or with the practice's operational and strategic goals.

Overreliance on Historical Data

Although prior year amounts and other historical data are often useful in estimating budget amounts, practices need to avoid relying too heavily on retrospective data. Those involved in the budget process need to consider how known and anticipated changes in the practice and the marketplace in general will affect these amounts. For example, changes in fee schedules, payer mix, and the local economy impact net revenues. The addition of a physician or a new location will impact revenues, as well as many costs. The budget should address inflation and significant increases in costs, such as employee health insurance. Finally, budget personnel need to consider whether historical numbers reflect waste and inefficiencies.

Budgetary Slack

Managers sometimes hedge against adversity by submitting easily obtainable budget amounts, especially when personnel evaluations are based largely upon adhering to the budget, or when across-the-board cost reductions are anticipated.[4] One estimate holds that, for traditionally managed organizations, the cost of inefficiency and waste is between 20 percent and 40 percent of budget.[5]

The danger here is that budgetary slack misleads leaders about the true potential of the practice. To guard against budgetary slack, administrators may benchmark submitted budget amounts against industry data. Zero-based budgeting (discussed earlier in this chapter) may also reduce the potential for budgetary slack.

Unattainable Budgets

While slack budgets rarely challenge managers, overly ambitious budgets also fail to motivate them. Because they offer little opportunity to avoid failure, unattainable budgets are more likely to increase anxiety than stimulate motivation or creative thinking. Unobtainable budgets do not provide realistic information. As a result, practice personnel do not take the budget process seriously, and the organization does not reap many of the potential benefits from the process.

Best Bet: The Challenging But Attainable Budget

Research indicates that budgets which are challenging, but attainable, improve performance. Jack Welch, the legendary former chief executive officer of General Electric, agrees – he claims challenging budgets energize and motivate managers, unleashing creative, out-of-the box thinking.[6]

■ Summary

Preparing a budget can assist a practice in attaining its short-term and long-term goals. Depending on its needs, structure, and other attributes, a practice's budget may actually include several budgets. These include, but are not limited to, the statistics budget, revenue budget, expense budget, staff budget, capital budget, cash budget, master budget, and departmental budgets.

Practice leaders need to ensure that they devote sufficient attention to the budget process. Budgets that are challenging, but attainable, often result in better performance than budgets that are unattainable or include slack. Finally, the organization needs to allow adequate time for department managers to develop accurate numbers and for the administrator or other budget coordinator to resolve conflicts among preliminary budget amounts and synchronize them with the practice's strategic and operational goals.

Chapter 2 **Establishing Processes for Cash Management and External Audits**

There's no business like show business, but there are several businesses like accounting.

— DAVID LETTERMAN

AN ACCOUNTING SYSTEM PROVIDES THE BASIC STRUCTURE for accumulating the practice's financial information. The amounts contained in financial statements and tax returns come from the accounting system. Historical information from the accounting system may be used to determine the amounts used in prospective statements, such as budgets and forecasts. Even if a practice uses zero-based budgeting and derives its budget from scratch, it still compares this budget against actual data from the accounting system.

The accounting system does not just provide information for financial reporting, it also supplies much of the information used for management decision making. For example, determining the break-even point or computing the cost of sending out a bill involves using data from the accounting system. The information used to compute physician bonuses or track expense accounts also comes from the accounting system.

This chapter discusses the fundamentals of how an accounting system accumulates financial information. It also provides an overview of management accounting and cost accounting, which use accounting system data. Finally, because the practice must safeguard its accounting system and the practice's assets, this chapter discusses internal controls.

◼ The Accounting System

An accounting system begins with a chart of accounts, which categorizes the various transactions that are recorded through payroll, accounts payable, the revenue cycle, and other sources. The transactions are then posted to the general ledger, which lists the activity for each account number in the chart of accounts and maintains the balance of cumulative activity for each account. The amounts from the general ledger provide the basis for the financial statements, tax returns, and many financial analyses.

Chart of Accounts

The chart of accounts provides the basic framework for organizing and classifying accounting transactions. It can be simple or complex, according to the needs of the organization.

The Numbering System

In addition to a basic numbering system, a chart of accounts may contain additional digits indicating location, division, or other attributes. For example, a practice may include identifying digits to track the professional expenses of the individual physicians and key personnel.

The basic chart. The core digits in a chart of accounts are the ones that identify its basic description. "Furniture and fixtures" and "travel" are examples of descriptions that might identify the core section of a chart of accounts numbers.

The order of a chart of account's core digits generally follows the financial statement order, with the balance sheet accounts first and the income statement accounts second. For example, the

EXHIBIT 9

Basic Field – Financial Categories
(from MGMA/HFMA Chart of Accounts)[7]

Account Number	Description
1000	Assets
2000	Liabilities
3000	Owners' equity
4000	Revenues
4500	Adjustments & allowances
5000	Operating expenses – salaries & fringe benefits
6000-7000	Services & general expense
8000	Provider-related expenses
9000	Nonoperating revenues & expenses; income taxes & other expenses

Reprinted with permission of MGMA.

Medical Group Management Association (MGMA) and the Healthcare Financial Management Association (HFMA) have developed a chart of accounts that contains the basic account numbering system as shown in Exhibit 9.

The first digit in the basic field indicates the major financial statement category. The second digit more specifically classifies the account by indicating a subcategory within the major category. For example, Exhibit 10 shows the second digit classification of the balance sheet or statement of financial position accounts.

This chart of accounts uses the additional digits in the basic field to further refine the attributes of a particular account.

Additional fields. A chart of accounts may also refine the definition of a particular account by adding additional fields to its basic chart. For example, a practice may add an additional field identifying the particular location and/or department connected with a specific account. A practice might also use a supplemental field to track expenditures relating to a specific physician. For example, a practice's account mask might look like this: XXXX.LL.PP. In this

EXHIBIT 10
Statement of Financial Position (Balance Sheet) Accounts
(from MGMA/HFMA Chart of Accounts)[8]

Account Number	Description
1000	Assets
1100-1500	Current assets
1600	Investments and long-term receivables
1700-1800	Noncurrent tangible assets
1900	Intangible and other assets
2000	Liabilities
2100-2300	Current liabilities
2400	Long-term liabilities
3000	Owners' equity

Reprinted with permission from MGMA.

example, "XXXX" represents the basic field, "LL" the location field, and "PP" the physician identifier field. Assuming Dr. Green is physician "05," works at the East End Clinic (location "02"), and the basic account number for physician meetings is "8255," the cost of Dr. Green's meetings would be charged to account 8255.02.05.

A practice usually uses the "00" field for expenditures that it cannot attribute to a particular location, department, or physician.

Other Considerations in Setting Up a Chart of Accounts

Using a standard chart of accounts can ease the process and provide a tested framework for setting up a practice's chart of accounts. Standard charts of accounts include the MGMA/HFMA chart of accounts and those provided by accounting firms and software vendors.

The MGMA/HFMA chart, designed specifically for health care organizations, is flexible enough that it can be used by a variety of practices. This chart is designed to facilitate completing MGMA cost surveys and benchmarking against MGMA survey data.

Certified public accountant (CPA) firms often maintain a standard chart of accounts that they copy when creating a chart of accounts for a new client. Often these charts of accounts are flexible enough to be used throughout a wide variety of industries, including medical practices. Accounting firms might also have industry-specific standard charts of accounts. When working with a new client, it is easier for a CPA to use a standard chart of accounts than create a new chart from scratch. If the CPA firm maintains the practice's general ledger and prepares its financial statements, the practice can save staff time at the firm (and hopefully lower accounting fees) by using the firm's standard chart of accounts. However, using a standard chart of accounts that is not specific to physician practices can result in a loss of valuable data, as well as an inability to compare the data to national benchmarks.

Accounting software vendors sometimes include sample charts of accounts with the purchase of software. Using the vendor's chart of accounts often makes setting up the accounting system easier and less time-consuming.

Whether using a chart of accounts from MGMA/HFMA, the practice's accounting firm, a software vendor, or one designed from scratch, the practice needs to devote sufficient time and resources to customizing this chart to meet its needs. A well-planned chart can facilitate better financial reporting, tax reporting, and management's ability to extract the data from the accounting system that it needs for decision making. A chart that is easy to set up or used by a variety of industries may be too basic to meet a practice's needs for extracting data from its system. A poorly designed chart can make the financial reporting and decision-making process unnecessarily cumbersome and time-consuming for those who assemble the data.

On the other hand, a chart that is unnecessarily complex involves excessive time and resources to process accounting transactions. A tricky part of planning the chart is making it complex enough to provide good information for reporting and decision making, flexible enough to accommodate growth and change, and simple enough to eliminate unnecessary work for the accounting staff.

Recording Transactions: Journals, Modules, and Journal Entries

A practice engages in many financial transactions, all of which its accounting system should properly reflect. The accounting system needs to provide a mechanism for assigning the appropriate chart of accounts code to each of these transactions. Most transactions first enter the accounting system through what have historically been referred to as "journals," but are often referred to as "modules" in today's era of computerized accounting systems. Common journals or modules used by medical practices include payroll and accounts payable. Practices that carry significant quantities of medical supplies, drugs, or items for resale (i.e., glasses, lenses, or orthopedic devices) might also use an inventory module.

Accounting System Modules: Setup Considerations

When setting up an accounting system, practice personnel typically make decisions that control how transactions are classified. For example, when setting up payroll, the practice can generally specify the accounts to which certain payroll transactions post. Accounting systems often permit transactions to post in either detail or summary form. Posting in detail, the general ledger contains the details of the individual transactions. For example, the office-supplies account lists all of the individual invoices for office supplies rather than just the total of all invoices for the period. The advantage of summary posting is that the general ledger is smaller, and the disadvantage is that staff may need to go to the subsidiary records to obtain specific details. Some accounting systems have a "drilldown" feature that offers the best of both worlds; it is a condensed general ledger that provides details with the click of a mouse.

Accounting Personnel: Understanding Chart of Accounts Methodology Is Crucial

Because some of the decisions regarding chart of accounts coding are made on an ongoing basis, personnel who routinely use these modules should be familiar with the chart of accounts and its methodology. For example, although the accounts payable module often has a default chart of accounts code for each vendor, the appropriate account number often varies. A check written to a specific physician could be reimbursement for a meeting, entertainment expense, office supplies, or some other purpose. The addition of a new employee to the payroll module usually involves assigning an account for that employee's salary, for example, "salaries–billing" or "salaries–laboratory."

Even if a practice's outside accountant maintains the general ledger and prepares the financial statements, its administrator or other financial personnel usually need to be familiar with the chart of accounts. They are often responsible for communicating the proper chart of accounts codes for practice transactions to the accountant. Practice personnel also need to extract data from the ledger to perform financial analysis.

General Journal Entries: Recording Other Transactions

Although these modules or journals often produce the bulk of a practice's accounting transactions, the accounting system must have a mechanism for recording other financial transactions. The book or worksheets that contain entries of these transactions are referred to as the "general journal."

A practice usually records depreciation on its fixed assets or its retirement plan accrual through a journal entry. It might also use a journal entry to correct the account number to which a particular transaction was charged. A practice that outsources its payroll can record summary payroll information with a general journal entry.

Transferring Revenue Cycle Data to the Accounting System

Most practices use a practice management system to bill charges and manage accounts receivable. Some practices have an interface between their practice management system and their accounting system, which allows billing activity to post automatically to the general ledger. Other practices record billing, collections, and other accounts receivable information through a journal entry. The billing system can usually produce a report that summarizes the information necessary to make the journal entry. The nature in which the practice records this data varies significantly depending on whether the practice is a cash basis or accrual basis practice.

General Ledger

The general ledger lists activities for each account in the chart of accounts. This information comes from other journals or modules, such as the payroll, accounts payable, or the general journal. The process of transferring or entering this activity in the general ledger is referred to as "posting." In addition to containing a list of activities, each account has a "balance" at any given point in time. All transactions either increase or decrease this balance. Accounting systems use "debits" and "credits" to signify whether a particular transaction increases or decreases an account's balance. A debit increases the balance of an asset or expense account, whereas a credit decreases the balance of these accounts. Conversely, credits increase liability, equity, and revenue accounts, whereas debits decrease these accounts.

Asset and expense accounts normally have a debit balance, whereas liability, equity, and income accounts normally have a credit balance. This is referred to as the account's "normal" balance. When reviewing the general ledger, the administrator and other practice personnel should be alert for accounts that do not have a normal balance. For example, a credit balance in cash indicates an overdraft. A debit balance in a liability account indicates a potential overpayment. Balances that are not "normal" may indicate accounting errors that need to be corrected.

Exhibit 11 shows, for the major financial statement classifications, whether a debit or credit increases or decreases the account and the "normal" account balance.

Finally, for every accounting transaction, the debits should equal the credits. Consequently, the sum of the account balances should equal zero. When the general ledger totals do not equal zero, it is out of balance, and the financial statements will also be out of balance. Accounting personnel will need to find the error and make appropriate corrections.

Financial Statement Preparation

The amounts on a practice's balance sheet and its income statement come directly from its general ledger. Often, the balances of similar

EXHIBIT 11

The Effect of Debits and Credits on Major Financial Statement Classifications

Financial Statement Classification	Increase	Decrease	Normal Balance
Asset	Debit	Credit	Debit
Liability	Credit	Debit	Credit
Equity	Credit	Debit	Credit
Income	Credit	Debit	Credit
Expense	Debit	Credit	Debit

accounts are combined to create one line item on the financial statements. For example, a practice may have several cash accounts, but only one amount for cash on its balance sheet.

To prepare the statement of cash flows, accounting personnel must go beyond the general ledger and analyze cash flow and/or other account activity. Preparing the statement of changes in equity may also involve additional analysis.

The Closing Process

At the end of the accounting year, practice personnel should expand upon normal month-end procedures to ensure that ending balances are correct. For example, while a practice may record an estimated provision for depreciation on a monthly basis, it should ensure the final depreciation balance matches the amount on its updated depreciation schedule. If the practice has an outside accountant report on the year-end financial statements, it will need to post any adjustments the accountant may have to the general ledger.

In order to close its books for the year, a practice must adjust all income statement accounts to zero and transfer the balance of these accounts (which is the practice's profit or loss for the year) to an equity account. (For a corporation, this account is retained earnings.) Most computerized systems perform this function automatically when selecting a year-end closing option, although the practice may need to stipulate the specific equity account(s) to which the transfer should be made.

After completing the closing process, the practice is ready to record transactions for the next year. All income statement accounts begin the year with a zero balance, while the ending balance sheet amounts for the old year will be the beginning balances for the new year. This is because the balance sheet reflects amounts at a point in time, whereas the income statement reports the totals for a period in time.

Depreciation

Practices often acquire long-term assets in the course of their business operations. Although these assets have expected useful lives of greater than one year, most of these assets (other than land) will not last forever. The practice needs a mechanism for spreading the cost of these assets over their expected useful lives. This mechanism is depreciation. During each year of the asset's estimated life, the practice recognizes a portion of the asset's cost as an expense and reduces the net value of the asset on the balance sheet accordingly.

Although various methods for computing depreciation exist, the method a particular practice uses depends largely on its method of accounting and applicable tax rules at the time.

Straight-Line Depreciation

Straight-line depreciation spreads an asset's cost evenly over its expected useful life. Assuming related revenue flows are relatively constant during this period, this method is appropriate.

Accelerated Depreciation Methods

Accelerated depreciation methods expense larger amounts of the asset cost in the early years of the asset's life and correspondingly lower amounts in later years. The *double-declining balance method* recognizes depreciation at twice the straight-line rate based on the asset's *book value* (cost less accumulated depreciation). The *150-percent declining balance method* depreciation recognizes depreciation at one and one-half times the straight-line rate based on the asset's book value. The *sum-of-the-year's digits method* computes a decreasing amount of depreciation each year based on the fractions based upon the sum of the digits in the number of years of an asset's life. For example, the depreciation of an asset with an estimated useful life of five years is: 5/ (5+4+3+2+1) or 5/15 the first year, 4/15 the second year, and so on.

An accelerated depreciation method makes economic sense when the bulk of an asset's production comes in the early years of its life, thus better matching expenses with the related revenue.

Units-of-Production Depreciation

The *units-of-production* method of depreciation expenses the production for the year as a percentage of the total expected production during the asset's life. This depreciation method was developed to ensure matching of an asset's expense with the revenue generated. It is appropriate when the practice expects an asset's production to vary during its useful life.

Tax Depreciation

Income tax rules generally allow the use of accelerated depreciation methods for tangible personal property, such as medical and office equipment. Allowable methods under the General Depreciation System version of the Modified Accelerated Cost Recovery System allow for a 200-percent or 150-percent declining balance method that switches to straight-line depreciation when this amount provides a greater or equal deduction.[9] In recent years, tax laws have allowed qualifying taxpayers to expense the cost of qualifying asset additions up to a certain dollar amount in the year of acquisition. (The general limitation for 2006 was $108,000.[10]) This is referred to as a Section 179 deduction. Recent laws have also provided for bonus depreciation on certain assets. Many practices have taken advantage of these accelerated methods to save income taxes.

In addition to specifying certain depreciation methods, the tax laws contain guidance as to the useful lives for various types of assets. This information is available in IRS Publication 946.

Book vs. Tax Depreciation

Although tax rules generally permit all qualifying taxpayers to take accelerated depreciation on applicable assets, generally accepted accounting principles (GAAP) require that depreciation be economically reasonable; consequently, many accrual basis practices use a less aggressive depreciation method for book purposes. Differing book and tax depreciation methods contribute to the potential for deferred income taxes on accrual basis balance sheets.

Because cash method practices often use the same depreciation method for book purposes that they use for income tax purposes, the depreciation expense and resulting net income amounts reported on the practice's financial statements may fluctuate significantly. Although accelerated methods may not represent economic reality, they are allowable for tax purposes and usually reduce a practice's income tax liability. Consequently, practices generally use them for tax purposes.

◾ Financial Accounting vs. Management Accounting

Although financial accounting deals with external reporting to parties such as creditors, management accounting focuses on providing information to management for internal decision making.

Financial accounting must comply with specific external guidelines, such as GAAP or some other comprehensive basis of accounting. This ensures that the practice's financial statements are comparable with financial statements produced by other entities, so that an external party who is knowledgeable in financial reporting will understand the financial statements. The entries in a practice's general ledger generally conform to the basis of accounting that the practice uses for financial reporting purposes.

Unlike financial accounting, management accounting does not have a strict set of guidelines. Although accounting textbooks suggest approaches for providing this information, these approaches are not requirements. An organization has the flexibility to provide its management accounting information in the manner that best facilitates its internal decision making.

The practice's accounting system provides information for both financial accounting and management accounting.

◢ Cost Accounting

Cost accounting "measures and reports financial and nonfinancial information relating to the cost of acquiring or utilizing resources in an organization."[11] It supplies information for both financial accounting and management accounting.[12] Although administrators sometimes use the term *cost accounting* to refer to cost allocation, the field of cost accounting is much more comprehensive. Cost accounting textbooks usually include numerous other topics, such as budgets and projections, inventory management, computing return on investment, and short-term decision making (discussed in the following section).

Short-Term Decision Making

The cost accounting model for short-term decision making is cost-volume-profit analysis, which includes break-even analysis. To understand this model, one must first understand cost behavior, including the difference between fixed and variable costs and how changes in volume affect these costs. Cost-volume-profit analysis seeks to answer the question "what if" by analyzing how changes in fixed costs, variable cost per unit, price per unit, and volume affect profit. The components of cost-volume-profit analysis can form an algebraic equation that determines a practice's break-even point.

Cost Behavior: Fixed vs. Variable Costs

Fixed costs remain the same in total during a period of time, despite a large range of potential activity (referred to as the "relevant range"). For example, a practice's rent expense generally remains the same whether the physicians see no patients or have a packed schedule.

Other examples of fixed costs include malpractice insurance and certain staff costs, such as the administrator's base salary.

Variable costs vary directly with the practice's volume. For example, a practice's medical supplies expense generally increases in proportion to its volume. Suppose a practice's medical supplies cost runs $1 per office visit. If the practice sees no patients, it incurs no medical supplies expense. If it sees 1,000 patients, it incurs $1,000 medical supplies expense; if it sees 10,000 patients, it incurs $10,000 medical supplies expense, and so on.

A hybrid type of cost is the step-fixed cost. These costs remain the same over various ranges of activity, but increase by discrete amounts, or "steps," as the level of activity changes from one range to the next. Many staff costs are step-fixed costs.

Cost-Volume-Profit Analysis

Cost-volume-profit analysis studies the effect that changes in volume, selling price per unit, variable cost per unit, and fixed costs have on revenues, costs, and net income from operations. Exhibit 12 provides examples of changes in each of these variables.

EXHIBIT 12

The Cost-Volume-Profit Analysis Variables

Variable	Example of Changes
Selling price	▪ Change in payer fee schedule ▪ Improved collection of co-pays
Volume	▪ Increase in number of patients ▪ Increase in number of procedures per patient
Variable cost per unit	▪ Decrease in cost of medical supplies (i.e., from getting competitive bids) ▪ Increase in cost of linen service
Fixed cost	▪ Increase in rent ▪ Decrease in malpractice insurance (i.e., from finding a new carrier)

EXHIBIT 13

The Cost-Volume-Profit Formula

Financial accounting model	Revenues − expenses = profit
Basic cost-volume-profit model	Revenues − fixed costs − variable costs = profit
Cost-volume-profit formula	(Volume × sales price per unit) − fixed costs − (volume × variable costs per unit) = profit

Using these variables, the income statement equation can be restated as a cost-volume-profit formula. See Exhibit 13.

Note that the total revenues and the total variable costs both depend on volume, whereas fixed costs remain the same regardless of the volume. This means that for each additional unit of volume, the bottom line will change by the difference between the sales price per unit and the variable cost per unit. This amount is called the contribution margin; it can be expressed as either an amount per unit, a percentage, or in total.

After volume reaches a certain level, the total contribution margin is sufficient to cover the fixed costs. See Exhibit 14. level is called the break-even point. After reaching the break-even point, each additional unit of volume creates incremental profit equal to the contribution margin per unit.

Conducting break-even analyses helps a practice understand its current financial structure and facilitates short-term decision making. The break-even point can be computed in either units or in net revenues. See Exhibit 15.

A practice can use break-even analyses to compute the volume or net revenues required to achieve certain levels of profit by increasing fixed costs by the amount of desired profit.

The case study in Exhibit 16 illustrates break-even and cost-volume-profit analysis for a hypothetical radiology practice.[13]

EXHIBIT 14

Contribution Margin

Contribution Margin	Formula
Contribution margin per unit	Selling price per unit – variable cost per unit
Contribution percentage	(Selling price per unit – variable cost per unit)/ selling price per unit
Total contribution margin	Total selling price – total variable costs

Exhibit 17 displays break-even analysis for Big Valley Radiology in graph form. The arrow indicates the profit range.

Break-Even Analysis Under Capitation

The above discussion assumes the practice is compensated based on fee-for-service or discounted fee-for-service contracts. When practice revenues are derived from capitation, the amount of revenue is no

EXHIBIT 15

Break-Even Analysis Formula

Break-Even Point	Formula
In units	$BEPQ = FC/CMU$
In net revenues	$BEPR = FC/CM\%$

Definitions:
  $BEPQ$ = break-even point in quantity
  $BEPR$ = break-even point in net revenues
  FC = total fixed costs
  CMU = contribution margin per unit
  $CM\%$ = contribution margin percentage

longer based on volume of services provided. Capitation revenue is computed on the number of members for which the practice is responsible regardless of the services provided to the members. The actual revenue under capitation is the number of members for the month times the "per member per month" rate. Like fixed costs, capitated revenues remain the same regardless of volume. Thus, for capitation, the only variable that changes with volume is variable costs. Thus, the capitation model is profitable until variable costs increase to the point that they exceed net revenues, less fixed costs.

EXHIBIT 16

Big Valley Radiology Break-Even Analysis Example

Big Valley Radiology has experienced a 1.5-percent Medicare cut. Because its other payers "benchmark" off Medicare, this cut affects all of its reimbursement. The following table shows the practice's summary financial information before and after the cut.

Description	Before	Change	After
Net Revenue	$5,000,000	$(75,000)	$4,925,000
Fixed Overhead	1,570,000		1,570,000
Variable Overhead	280,000		280,000
Total Amount Distributable to Physicians	3,150,000	(75,000)	3,075,000
Profitability Per Physician	$450,000	(10,714)	$439,286
Number of Procedures	110,000		110,000
Number of FTE Physicians	7		7

Note that this is a change in sales price (reimbursement). Because the practice's volume was unaffected, variable costs remain the same in total. In computing revised break-even analysis, the decrease in sales price (reimbursement) decreased the contribution margin.

Description	Before	Change	After
Contribution Margin	$4,720,000	(75,000)	$4,645,000
Contribution Margin per Unit	$42.91	$(.68)	$42.23
Contribution Margin Percent	94.40%	$(.08)	94.32%

EXHIBIT 16 *(continued)*
Big Valley Radiology Break-Even Analysis Example

COMPUTING BREAK-EVEN POINT IN QUANTITY

The following example uses break-even analysis to compute the number of additional procedures the group must perform to maintain the same profitability per FTE physician it had prior to the increase.

BEPQ = FC/CMU
      (Breakeven Point in Quantity = Fixed Costs/Contribution Margin per Unit)

- Fixed Costs = Desired Profitability + Fixed Overhead
  $3,150,000 + $1,570,000 = $4,720,000

- CMU = RU – VCU
  (Contribution Margin per Unit = Revenue per Unit – Variable Costs per Unit)
  □ Revenue per Unit = $4,925,000/110,000 = $44.77
  □ Variable Cost per Unit = $280,000/110,000 = $2.54
  CMU = $44.77 - $2.54 = $42.23

BEPQ = $4,720,000 /$42.23 = 111,769

The group must perform 1,769 more procedures to make up for the Medicare cuts.

COMPUTING BREAK-EVEN POINT IN REVENUES

The following example uses break-even analysis to compute the additional revenue level the group must achieve to maintain the same profitability per FTE physician it had prior to the Medicare pay cut.

BEPR = FC/CM%
      (Breakeven Point in Revenues = Fixed Costs/Contribution Margin %)

- Fixed Costs = Desired Profitability + Fixed Overhead
  $4,720,000 (same as above example)

- Contribution Margin % = Contribution Margin per Unit/ Revenue per Unit
  $42.23/ $44.77 = 94.32%

BEPR = $4,720,000 / .9432 = $5,004,241

The group needs to increase its revenues $79,241 to make up for the 1.5% Medicare (and total reimbursement) cut.

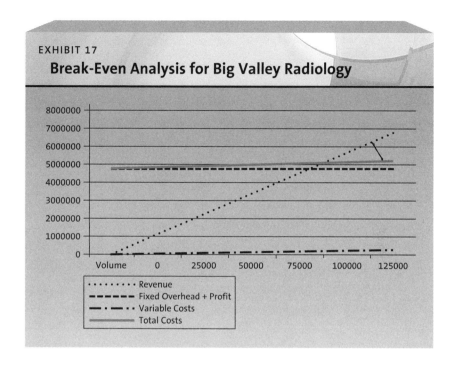

EXHIBIT 17

Break-Even Analysis for Big Valley Radiology

Legend:
- ········· Revenue
- ― ― ― ― Fixed Overhead + Profit
- ― · ― · · Variable Costs
- ━━━━━ Total Costs

Exhibit 18 shows the break-even graph for Big Valley Radiology assuming that all revenue is capitated.

Cost Allocation

Sometimes obtaining the information necessary to facilitate economic decision making requires cost allocation. For example, a practice may allocate costs to help determine whether a specific location is profitable, evaluate a proposed contract, or set its fee schedule. Many physician compensation plans require cost allocation.

A popular cost accounting textbook defines cost allocation as the "assignment of indirect costs to a particular cost object"[14] and a cost object as "anything for which a measurement of costs is desired."[15] Direct costs are those that can be traced to a cost object in a cost-effective manner. Conversely, indirect costs cannot be traced to a particular cost object in a cost-effective manner.[16]

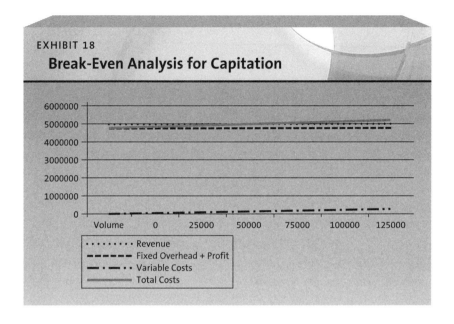

EXHIBIT 18
Break-Even Analysis for Capitation

For example, in computing the profit or loss for a satellite office, an administrator can easily trace the rent for that office and the salaries of its employees to that particular satellite office. These expenses are considered direct costs. The costs of a central administrative office pertain to multiple locations and cannot be easily traced to a particular clinic; these are indirect costs that must be allocated.

Cost accounting textbooks contain many different cost accounting models, some of which are quite complex. The best model for a particular situation depends on the industry, the attributes of the business and its owners, and the facts and circumstances of the particular situation. Exhibit 19 lists some of the methods commonly used to allocate costs in a medical practice and situations in which these models might be appropriate.

One challenge of cost allocation is the lack of a correct or incorrect answer to each scenario. The decision requires an understanding of cost allocation methodology, cost behavior, the specific problem, and the individual practice. It also requires judgment and a commitment to fairness.

Other (Unlimited) Uses of Cost Accounting

The true scope of cost accounting is infinite; management may incorporate measurement of many different costs in whatever format best facilitates decision making. By studying and practicing traditional management and cost accounting approaches, administrators can improve their ability to create special reports and recognize when situation-specific analyses might benefit their practice. Other methods for improving cost accounting skills include being alert for situations in which such analyses might be useful, discussions with colleagues about how they use cost accounting in their practice, and learning by doing – actually performing these analyses.

EXHIBIT 19

Cost Allocation Methods in a Medical Practice

Method	Situation in Which This Method Might Be Appropriate
Square footage	Allocating rent and utility costs to departments
Full-time-equivalent count	Allocating human resource management department costs
Payroll costs	Allocating workers' compensation insurance costs
Percentage of revenues	Allocating billing costs to divisions or locations
Volume – may be measured by number of procedures, charges, or relative value units	Allocating variable costs such as medical supplies, linens, and scheduling costs
Usage	Allocating information technology department costs based on the number of computers
Stipulated or agreed-upon percentage	Based on compromise or agreement among the group, particularly when no one method clearly reflects economic reality – for example, a practice might allocate a specific percentage of fixed expenses to a part-time physician
	For simplification – for example, a practice may assign administrative costs to individual clinics based on a stipulated percentage for interim purposes

◾ Internal Control

In the early 1990s, a group of accounting and financial organizations (called the Committee of Sponsoring Organizations of the Treadway Commission [COSO]) commissioned a comprehensive study of internal control. This study, referred to as the COSO study, was the result of concerns over the accounting scandals of the 1970s and 1980s. This study defines internal control as follows:

> Internal control is a process, effected by an entity's board of directors, management and other personnel, designed to provide reasonable assurance regarding the achievement of objectives in the following categories:
>
> - Effectiveness and efficiency of operations.
> - Reliability of financial reporting.
> - Compliance with applicable laws and operations.[17]

Worth noting is that this definition holds that internal control is a *process* integrated into the organization's business activities, rather than a set of policies and procedures imposed by regulators and outside parties. Although outside auditors must evaluate the system of internal control, the internal control process is the responsibility of insiders – the board of directors, management, and other personnel.

Finally, internal control provides only reasonable assurance that the entity achieves its objections. It cannot guarantee this outcome. Poor judgment, collusion of two or more people, and the ability of management to override a system of internal control can prevent the organization from fulfilling its goals.

The COSO study determined that five interrelated components comprise internal control. These are:

1. The control environment;
2. Risk assessment;
3. Control activities, such as policies and procedures;

4. Information and communication; and

5. Monitoring.[18]

The Control Environment

Corporate culture impacts the effectiveness of an organization's control process. Integrity and ethical behavior begin at the top – the actions of managers, owners, and directors set the tone for the rest of the organization. For example, employees who see managers engage in fraudulent or self-serving activities may be more inclined to engage in these activities themselves.

In addition to exhibiting integrity and ethical behavior, individuals at all levels of the organization must be competent to perform their functions. It's not enough for the organization's people to want to do a good job; they must do a good job.

Risk Assessment

Before a practice establishes appropriate controls, it must determine the risks that might prevent it from reaching its objectives. This requires that the practice first establish its objectives. These objectives may be created internally (i.e., desired profitability) or imposed externally (i.e., proper disposal of hazardous materials). Leadership should review the objectives to ensure that they are consistent with the practice's capability and that they do not contradict each other.

Risk assessment should include both internal and external factors that can prevent the practice from achieving its objectives.[19] External factors might include increased competition, new legislation, or a natural disaster, such as Hurricane Katrina. Internal factors can include the quality of personnel, a disruptive physician, or pharmaceutical inventory with a high street value. For each of the identified risks, the practice should estimate the potential consequences, likelihood, and how to best manage the risk.

Finally, change impacts an organization's objectives and the environment in which it operates. Thus, a practice needs to be forward-looking in its risk assessment, provide a mechanism for identifying new risks, and reassess its risks on a regular basis.[20]

Control Activities

Control activities are the policies and procedures that an organization implements to address the risks that might prevent it from achieving its objectives. Common types of such controls include physical controls, reconciliations, segregation of duties, information system controls, and review of financial data.[21] The appropriateness and effectiveness of the controls depend on the nature of the practice and its personnel.

Physical Controls

Physical controls provide barriers to accessing assets. For example, a practice might lock its medical supplies and drugs in a closet and provide a key only to designated individuals. Most organizations keep cash locked in a safe or cash drawer.

Reconciliations

Reconciliations compare actual quantities against control records. For example, the practice might compare the actual quantity of medical supplies on hand against perpetual inventory records and investigate any differences. A group might compare the number of procedures billed for a service to the number of supply units expensed for that specific procedure. Cash drawers should be reconciled at least daily.

A bank reconciliation compares the balance per the bank with the balance per the accounting records and accounts for all differences, such as outstanding checks. A practice's cash account or bank account is one of the areas most susceptible to fraud. Because of the risk associated with bank accounts, it is imperative to perform timely bank reconciliations so that any banking irregularities can be detected quickly. Bank reconciliations have traditionally been done monthly, but the fact that this information is available online allows a practice to balance its bank account at almost any point in time. Due to today's large amounts of electronic deposits and debits, many practices need to reconcile this balance frequently. For example, practices may need to compare the amount actually deposited in the bank against a payer's electronic remittance information.

Segregation of Duties

By dividing the duties associated with a particular area among different people, a practice reduces the risk of inappropriate activities. This typically involves separating the responsibilities for authorizing a transaction, recording the transaction, and physically handling the related asset. For example, the employee who orders supplies should not open the mail (which contains the related invoices), pay bills, receive the supplies, or maintain custody of the key to the supply cabinet. The employee who opens the mail and makes the bank deposit should not post payments or enter adjustments to patient accounts.

Although a small practice with limited business office staff may have difficulty accomplishing sufficient segregation of duties, this is usually possible. Using a bank lockbox and receiving payments electronically can improve control over cash receipts by preventing staff members who record the related transactions from physically accessing the payments.

Having physician-owners or outside accountants perform some of the incompatible functions may accomplish sufficient segregation of duties. For example, assigning a physician-owner or outside accountant to receive an unopened bank statement and review it before giving it to accounting personnel provides a check over accounts payable and bank account activity. When the practice administrator or another employee with other responsibilities for deposits or checks performs the bank reconciliations, it is critical that someone else reviews them.

Practice administrators sometimes serve as authorized check signers for their practices. Although this works well in some practices, it may create poor segregation of duties if the administrator performs incompatible accounts payable or checking account functions. A dishonest administrator who signs checks and handles accounts payable record-keeping can misappropriate funds, particularly when this administrator also reconciles the bank account. Requiring dual signatures on all checks or on checks in excess of a certain minimum amount can also improve control over disbursements.

Although using a facsimile signature stamp may expedite check processing, it can also reduce the effectiveness of internal control because anyone who has access to the facsimile signature stamp has the ability to approve a transaction. If the employee who prepares accounts payables checks has access to the facsimile signature stamp, this person has the ability to authorize, account for, and physically handle cash disbursements.

A practice should seriously consider whether using a facsimile signature poses an internal control risk. The stamp should be locked up with access given only to those with the authority to approve cash disbursements and who have no incompatible cash or accounts payable responsibilities.

Information System Controls

Like most businesses today, almost all medical practices use computers to process information. Thus, information system controls are an important part of a practice's internal control process. For medical practices, information system controls are necessary not only to help meet financial and operational goals, they are also necessary to ensure compliance with Health Insurance Portability and Accountability Act (HIPAA) security rules.

Reviewing Data and Performing Analytical Procedures

By reviewing data and performing analytical procedures, management can identify unusual results or trends. Examples include:

- Performance indicators, such as days in accounts receivable, payroll ratio, and other benchmarks;

- Top level reviews, such as comparing actual performance against budgets, forecasts, prior periods, and industry data; and

- Reviewing activity performance reports, for example, the billing manager reviews the various reports generated by the billing system on a daily, weekly, and monthly basis.

Identifying problem areas may enable management to take the corrective action necessary to help the organization achieve its objectives.

Information and Communication

The practice needs to ensure that it has information systems necessary to capture the internal and external information required to manage and control its operations. It also needs to effectively communicate information regarding and affecting the internal control process to employees and other stakeholders. For example, job descriptions communicate an employee's duties and responsibilities.

The practice should ensure effective communication across the organization. For example, employees at all levels might notice problems that can prevent an organization from meeting its objectives. The organization should provide a mechanism for all employees to communicate this information to management, including timely response to concerns expressed by employees and other stakeholders.

Monitoring

The practice should monitor its internal control system to ensure that it is functioning properly. Monitoring can be accomplished by ongoing activities and separate evaluations.

Many management activities, such as review of financial or operational data and being alert to what occurs in the practice on a day-to-day basis, are ongoing monitoring activities. Other ongoing monitoring activities are regular reports on the system of internal control (completed by internal or external auditors) and periodic statements by personnel regarding the code of conduct, compliance, and other issues affecting internal control.

Insiders or outsiders should perform separate evaluations and approach these activities as a "fresh look" rather than as a regular audit or ongoing review of an existing process. Examples of separate evaluation methodologies are checklists, questionnaires, flowcharts, and matrix analyses.

One tool that has been developed since the COSO study is the control self-assessment (CSA). This methodology, developed by CPA firms and some of the professional organizations that sponsored the COSO study, is a tool for insiders to use to evaluate their organization's internal control. The Institute of Internal Auditors offers CSA certification and has developed extensive literature and information about this process. One survey of organizations that had performed

CSA found that they often achieved process improvements as a by-product of the CSA, confirming the COSO view of internal control as a process.[22]

The scope and frequency of separate evaluations will depend on the practice's risks and other attributes. For example, the COSO study indicated that special evaluations may not be as necessary in smaller and midsize organizations. In these organizations, management is typically more involved in the day-to-day operations and is therefore more likely to become aware of internal control problems on an informal basis.[23]

Auditing Systems

The complexity of coding and documenting services makes it likely that providers may at times miscode services at a higher or lower level than what is considered proper, or fail to provide enough documentation to justify the code selected. Downcoding, which is entering a lower-than-appropriate code, causes lower reimbursements and skews measurements of provider productivity. Coding at a higher-than-justified level – upcoding – can lead payers to suspect fraud. The repercussions can include payer audits of the practice's records, or worse, civil or criminal charges against the provider and possible suspension or exclusion from the payer's program. Therefore, it is critical that administrators implement a voluntary program of compliance with federal billing and coding requirements. The Office of Inspector General for Health and Human Services, which has the authority to exclude providers from the Medicare and Medicaid programs, recommends that a practice routinely review bills and medical notes for compliance with coding, billing, and documentation requirements.

When initiating a compliance program, the practice must determine whether to review claims retrospectively or concurrently as they are submitted.[24] The auditing system can begin with a baseline audit, only examining claims submitted during the three-month period immediately after the compliance program begins. Follow-up audits should be conducted at least annually to ensure that the practice's compliance program is being followed. At a minimum, the practice should review the claims it has submitted for reimbursement from federal programs. One of the most important components of an audit protocol is making an appropriate response when a problem is detected. This may include refunding overpayments to payers, implementing compliance standards, increasing provider education, and, in cases of deliberate miscoding, enforcing disciplinary actions.

Resource-Based Relative Value Scale

Government programs and most private payers use the resource-based relative value scale (RBRVS) as the basis for physician payment. The RBRVS assigns relative values to most of the Current Procedural Terminology (CPT®) codes. The values are based on the resources that a physician typically uses to perform the service. The resources are divided into three parts:

- Physician work – time, technical skill, physical strength, mental effort and judgment, physician stress, and total work;

- Practice expenses – rent, support staff, supplies, and other items that may vary with the physician's gross revenue, mix of services, and practice location; and

- Malpractice expenses – costs that vary by specialty.

The RBRVS uses relative values – nonmonetary, relative units of measure – for approximately 8,000 of the CPT-4 codes. It converts these relative values into dollar amounts by applying a conversion factor. The Medicare program uses a single conversion factor that it updates annually in the Medicare Fee Schedule. Then a geographic component adjusts the payments according to regional differences in the cost of living and physician practice costs. Private insurance carriers tend to use different conversion factors.

Although the RBRVS was developed as a reimbursement mechanism, the data can be used in other ways. Because relative value units (RVUs) summarize the relative weight of procedures performed by physicians for all patients, regardless of the payer or the physician's charges, administrators can use them to evaluate how much an individual physician's activities contribute to practice profits.

Administrators can also use RVUs to estimate the cost of services provided or determine a physician's compensation.

To develop its own RVUs, a practice can extract procedure code data from its billing system and relate those data to the relative value weights for each procedure as assigned by the Medicare RBRVS. The RVUs are calculated as follows:

Total Relative Value Units = Total Procedures Performed × Value Units*

Modifiers

After the correct CPT code or Healthcare Common Procedure Coding System code has been selected, the provider should determine whether a modifier should be appended to the code. Modifiers give payers additional information to process the claim, such as special circumstances about the service or procedure. It is important to know the effect that a modifier may have on how the claim is processed. Sometimes a modifier requires the provider to file additional documentation with the claim. Some modifiers may increase or decrease the reimbursement for the CPT code, while other modifiers simply communicate information. Each payer can set its own policies for when modifiers are applicable and what additional documentation must be provided.

Coding Resources (Specialty Specific)

The complexity of diagnosis and CPT-4 coding can vary greatly by physician specialty. For example, many of the procedure codes routinely used to describe anesthesia services are time based and require unique documentation. As a result, most medical specialty associations, and a number of for-profit publishers, provide extensive coding guidance resources, including printed and computerized guides, online resources, newsletters, educational resources, and other advice geared to their members' specialty. In addition, a number of coding consultants focus on certain specialties.

---

* Obtained from the Medicare RBRVS.

Risk Contracts (Capitation and Case Rates, Withholds)

Contracts between physicians and insurance companies take many forms. Capitation is a sophisticated type of risk contracting that is not widely used. A capitation contract pays the physician a fixed amount for each patient for whom the physician accepts responsibility. This fee, which is paid in advance each month, is known as the per-member-per-month (PMPM) amount and is expected to cover a specified range of service. Patients covered by these contracts are restricted to seeing only the physicians within a panel designated by the insurer. Physicians face great financial risk if more of their assigned patients end up using more of the services than the negotiated PMPM amount covers. Some managed care companies withhold a portion of the physician's PMPM fee in reserve to pay for any utilization in excess of the contracted fee, or to reward physicians who meet goals for access, quality, patient satisfaction, or control of medical costs. Capitation has been most frequently applied to limit the costs of and access to primary care physicians. There are many variations of the risk contract concept, including negotiating special fees for certain costly procedures or treatments that may include many different services. Similar to bundling, the insurance company groups various services together and pays the physician a flat rate, or case rate. In obstetrics, it is common to negotiate a case rate for a normal vaginal delivery and a case rate for a cesarean section, or blend the rate for both based on a formula of expected utilization.

Fee-for-Service and Contract Reimbursement Rates

The traditional approach to reimbursing physicians via fee-for-service insurance that paid the full amount of the physician's charges for services rendered is rarely seen these days. More commonly, physicians are paid under discounted fee-for-service contracts that discount the physician's full charge by an agreed-upon amount negotiated between the payer and physician or the physician's practice. These payments may also be based on a fee schedule specified in the contract between the physician and the insurance company. The insurance company's payment may be made to the patient who would then reimburse the physician. More commonly, the payment is reassigned by the patient to be sent directly to the physician practice. Contracts between physicians and insurance companies typically require the physician to accept the contracted amount of payment (except for any copayments or deductibles amount owed by the patient) as payment in full for the services rendered. These contracts also prevent physicians from billing patients for any difference between the contracted amount and the physician's full charge for the services rendered.[25]

Auditing Payments

Practices need to devote sufficient resources to ensure that the amounts of net revenue (fee-for-service revenue, capitation revenue, and any other revenues) in the financial statements are a reasonably accurate representation of the amounts the practice will ultimately collect.[26] Inadequately computing these amounts leads to a misleading financial statement that can overstate or understate the revenues on which physicians' bonuses or other compensation is computed. It may also cause the practice to run short of cash, miss instances of underpayment by payers and mistakes by outsourced billing companies, and, potentially, negotiate less-than-favorable fees in future contracts with insurance companies.

■ Regulatory Agency and Contract Guidelines and Mandates

Several federal agencies regulate the financial aspects of medical practice reimbursement from public insurance programs like Medicare and Medicaid. Private insurers also develop reimbursement guidelines that may vary from those of the public programs. In addition, several nonpublic agencies promulgate voluntary quality standards and accreditation requirements that the health care industry recognizes. These standards may influence private payers' and, increasingly, consumers' decisions to select a hospital or medical practice.

CMS

The Centers for Medicare and Medicaid Services (CMS), a federal agency within the U.S. Department of Health and Human Services, administers the Medicare and Medicaid programs that provide health insurance coverage to more than 75 million Americans. Formerly known as the Health Care Financing Administration (HCFA), the role of CMS in the regulatory oversight of physicians and other providers is significant because many physicians and hospitals accept Medicare beneficiaries and rely on those medical revenues. Because of the size of its insured population, the agency's rules and payment policies often set the tone for the policies of private insurance companies. Efforts by CMS to protect the fiscal integrity of its programs and ensure appropriate and predictable payments and high-quality care have led to many regulations of which the practice administrator must be aware. Violating these rules can result in fines, civil or criminal actions, and temporary or permanent expulsion from participating in Medicare and Medicaid programs, as well as from the State Children's Health Insurance Program, which CMS also administers. The agency is also responsible for overseeing the HIPAA administrative simplification transaction and code sets, health identifiers, and security standards.

Insurance

Private insurance companies may set payment policies within the broader outlines of state and federal regulations. The medical practice manager must ensure that the practice follows the reimbursement, coding, and collection policies of its many private insurance payers. Failure to abide by a private insurer's rules can result in denied claims, but may also bring other penalties, such as exclusion from that insurer's network or cancellation of its contracts with the provider. Private insurance companies may also seek civil action against providers who violate their billing and coding guideline rules. In cases where a payer suspects fraud, the payer may have grounds to seek civil or criminal prosecution by public authorities.

State

States create guidelines for health care quality and business practices through laws and regulations. These rules may affect the corporate structure of a medical practice as well as how it operates and what revenue opportunities it may explore. A state also may regulate the business practices of health insurance companies doing business in the state. In addition, states set scope of practice laws that determine what services nonphysician providers may provide to patients of a medical practice.

Healthcare Effectiveness Data and Information Set

The National Committee for Quality Assurance (NCQA) developed the Healthcare Effectiveness Data and Information Set (HEDIS). HEDIS is a tool that consists of a set of performance measures for managed care organizations. These measures, such as immunization and mammography screening rates, can show how well health plans perform in the areas of quality of care and access to care. HEDIS also measures member satisfaction with the health plan and its doctors. Health plans collect these data in a standardized manner and must have their HEDIS results verified by independent auditors. Although it is not mandated by law, the use of HEDIS has become a more widely accepted tool for health insurance purchasers to gauge the quality of care and service a health plan provides. More than half the nation's health maintenance organizations currently participate in order to gain an NCQA seal of approval, and close to 90 percent of all health plans measure performance using HEDIS.

National Committee for Quality Assurance

The National Committee for Quality Assurance (NCQA) is a private, not-for-profit organization that establishes standards of quality in management care plans and reports these outcomes to the public. To gain NCQA accreditation, a health plan must self-monitor its performance on the HEDIS measures that NCQA develops and take steps to improve performance. As a nongovernmental agency, the NCQA does not have legal power to discipline noncompliant organizations, but rather it can grant or withhold its accreditation. NCQA makes its assessments available on the Web (at www.healthchoices. org and www.ncqa.org) for employers and the public to make health care purchasing decisions. The organization plans to issue ratings of medical groups and individual physicians.

Joint Commission on Accreditation of Healthcare Organizations

The Joint Commission on Accreditation of Healthcare Organizations (JCAHO) is a not-for-profit organization that evaluates and accredits more than 15,000 health care organizations and programs in the United States. Its goal is to improve the quality and safety of care provided by health care organizations. Also known as "the Joint Commission," JCAHO's accreditation process evaluates an organization's compliance with standards and other accreditation requirements. Its voluntary evaluation and accreditation services are provided to hospitals, long- and short-term care facilities, home health care agencies, laboratories, group practices, ambulatory surgery centers, and organizations that deliver disease management and chronic care services. The accreditation process requires JCAHO inspections at least every three years.

Summary

All practices, whether large or small, need an accounting system to maintain the financial information necessary to meet both external reporting and internal decision-making needs.

External reporting must conform to accounting principles and tax laws, whereas internal reporting is more flexible – its format depends on the needs of the organization and the ability of the accounting system to generate information.

Finally, the practice needs appropriate processes to ensure that it meets its financial and operational goals and complies with applicable laws. This process is its system of internal control. Because controls over the accounting system and the organization's assets are key to meeting these objectives, internal control considerations are crucial components of a practice's accounting system.

Chapter 3 **Revenue Cycle and Accounts Receivable Management**

◼ Accounts Receivable Measurement/Management Systems

A MEDICAL PRACTICE'S MOST IMPORTANT FINANCIAL ASSET is its accounts receivables. Accounts receivable (A/R) represent amounts that have been billed to (but not yet paid by) patients and third-party payers such as insurance companies. A/R can also include amounts billed but not yet paid by other revenue sources, such as clinical trial sponsors, medical directorships, and so forth.

Accurately tracking and measuring these future monies allows a manager to understand how well the practice collects these funds, both in the aggregate and from each payment source. Tracking A/R also shows how various payment sources perform in relation to each other and to industry benchmarks. This tracking is more than an academic exercise because A/R represents money that is not yet collected and assets that cannot be used, except perhaps as collateral for loans. In most cases, A/R does not earn interest for the medical practice, which means that inflation and overhead costs are eroding the value of this asset for each day that it remains uncollected.

Poor management of A/R results in delayed collections, and sometimes in uncollectible claims that must be written off. Ultimately, poor management of A/R causes a shortage of the incoming cash on which the practice relies to pay staff and providers, service debt and other liabilities such as utilities, supplies, and so forth. Inaccurate tracking of A/R reduces the practice's ability to anticipate its future cash flow and spot ways to improve its coding, billing, and collections processes. Therefore, it is critical that new charges for services rendered are posted in a timely manner, billing is sent to payers and patients expeditiously, and revenues are reported accurately. Protocols must be created and enforced to conduct credit checks and investigations, when appropriate, and ensure accurate and clear billing and collection policies.

Aging

The medical practice must make a continuous effort to track the age of its A/R. Monitoring A/R by age can be an excellent indicator of how well the practice manages this asset. The practice manager and its owner/shareholders should routinely review reports that list A/R in the following categories: current–30 days, 31–60 days, 61–90 days, 91–120 days, more than 120 days, and total A/R. A computerized practice management system allows the practice to easily produce reports of A/R in these categories and also by payer source, patient, physician, specialty, department, and other classifications. Tracking these data over time, comparing A/R month to month or between the current month and the previous year, provides a useful picture of the practice's collections performance. These snapshots can help the administrator to understand and anticipate cash flow into the practice and spot any potential causes of uncollected debt.

Benchmarking

Benchmarking helps managers monitor and analyze the practice's financial and operational performance. Benchmarking data can be extracted from a variety of sources, but it most frequently comes from the practice's computerized management system. By measuring these data across time, internally among different people and processes, as well as against industry benchmarks, a practice manager can develop a clear road map for process improvement.[27] Several internal and external benchmarks are commonly tracked and analyzed for A/R. These benchmarks include total days in A/R and days receivables outstanding. Monitoring the practice's performance in days in A/R and the percent of A/R in various categories against benchmarks can also help administrators decide when to write off A/R as uncollectible.[28]

Net vs. Gross Revenue

Revenue – the inflow of assets, usually cash or receivables, in return for services rendered – increases the practice's net assets and the practice owners' equity. However, it is important to distinguish between net and gross revenue. In a medical practice, gross revenue is the amount expected to be received for services delivered to patients as well as from items, supplies, and other sources, such as the technical component of radiology procedures, margins from outpatient drugs, and other services. Subtracted from gross revenue are payers' contractual allowances, sliding fee discounts, and other adjustments.

Days Outstanding Collections

This important benchmark, also known as "days in accounts receivable" or "days in A/R," shows the practice's ability to manage this important asset and turn it into cash. It calculates the average number of days from the date of service to the collection of cash. The typical formula for calculating this benchmark is: total accounts receivable/(gross charges/days in period). Because the gross charge amount can vary significantly, depending on the physicians' fee schedule, the industry standard is to view the average daily charge over a year (365 days). This allows easier comparison to external benchmarks such as those provided in Medical Group Management Association® cost survey reports.

Coding Systems, Guidelines, and Resources

Payers, including the Medicare program, apply various payment guidelines to reimburse physicians for services they render to patients. These guidelines rely on published numerical codes that a provider enters on an electronic or paper encounter form to indicate the medical diagnosis and the resulting services, procedures, or supplies that are rendered. Practices must establish standards for proper documentation and coding to ensure that billing is accurate and complete. Improper coding and documentation can cause overpayments, underpayments, and denials of claims.

The authors of *The Physician Billing Process: Avoiding Potholes in the Road to Getting Paid*[29] suggest that to ensure coding standards are understood and followed, make the following resources readily accessible to providers, managers, and staff:

- The Current Procedural Terminology (CPT®) manual (updated each January);

- The diagnosis code (ICD-9-CM) manual and additional manuals for certain specialties (updated each October);

- The *HCFA Common Procedure Coding System (HCPCS)* manual (updated each January);

- Correct Coding Initiative edits (updated quarterly);

- A medical dictionary;

- Medicare and/or Medicaid regional carrier updates and any specialty billing guides (kept electronically or on paper in a binder);

- Insurance newsletters;

- Medical specialty publications; and

- Online access to the *Federal Register* (www.thomas.loc.gov), the Centers for Medicare and Medicaid Services (CMS) at www.cms.gov, the state Medicaid program Website, and insurance company Websites.

These sources and the purposes of these various guidelines are explained in the following sections.

CPT and ICD-9

Most payers, including CMS, which administers the Medicare program, process claims for medical services using *Current Procedural Terminology*, fourth edition (CPT-4), a coding structure developed, copyrighted, and maintained by the American Medical Association

(AMA). This manual assigns five-digit codes to medical services and procedures as a way to standardize claims processing and data analysis. CPT codes may have modifiers attached so the provider can provide more detail when needed. Although CPT-4 codes identify the medical services provided, they do not name payment amounts. Payers choose which codes they will reimburse, specify when those codes and modifiers are reimbursable, and set payment amounts for codes.

The HCPCS (Healthcare Common Procedure Coding System) is a standardized method used to report professional services, procedures, and supplies. HCPCS codes are typically paid on a flat rate and not assigned relative value units (relative measurements of work effort). HCPCS codes are used to identify services not fully described in the CPT-4 system, such as ambulance transportation, injections, durable medical equipment, and supplies. They are also used for new procedures not yet assigned CPT codes. Some HCPCS codes, also known as Level III HCPCS codes or "local codes," may be used in certain states or regions at the discretion of the regional Medicare carrier or the state's Medicaid program.

Payers also require physicians and other providers to supply one or more diagnosis codes to justify the procedures for which they are claiming reimbursement. The diagnosis codes, which are numeric with a few exceptions, are listed in the *International Classification of Diseases,* ninth revision, Clinical Modifications (ICD-9-CM). The National Center for Health Statistics and CMS oversee modifications of ICD-9-CM, which is based on an internationally agreed-upon methodology to track diseases and injuries. ICD-9-CM codes are three to five digits long, depending on the level of specificity. These codes identify diagnoses, symptoms, conditions, or other reasons for an encounter or visit. In addition, nonnumerical E codes may be used to report events that cause injury, and V codes are used to indicate health visits when the patient is not sick or has conditions related to general health status.

E/M Levels of Service

Evaluation and management (E/M) codes are listed in the AMA CPT-4 manual and tend to represent the cognitive services that physicians perform. The CPT-4 E/M codes apply to:

- Office visits;

- Hospital visits;

- Consultations;

- Emergency services;

- Critical care; and

- Other services, such as home services and case management.

Each of these areas has as many as five levels of care, from simple to complex. When these areas are fully documented, they reflect the physicians' work and help determine reimbursement amounts.

CMS has created documentation guidelines to help physicians understand how to apply codes for E/M services. These guidelines, which are not part of the CPT manual, require the physician to document seven components to determine the proper coding level of an E/M service:

1. History;

2. Examination;

3. Medical decision making;

4. Counseling;

5. Coordination of care;

6. Nature of presenting problem; and

7. Time.

The degree to which these components are satisfied helps determine, for example, whether an office visit is coded as a simple encounter (i.e., a CPT-coded 99211 visit) or a more complex (and likely a more highly reimbursed) encounter, such as a 99215.

CCI and Bundling Guidelines

Because of the complexity of coding and compliance concerns about its proper use, CMS implemented the Correct Coding Initiative (CCI) in 1996. Its goal is to reduce program costs by detecting inappropriate coding on Medicare claims and denying payment for them. Because the edits, which essentially are reasons for claims denials, are updated quarterly, medical practices must be diligent to keep up with the latest CCI additions, deletions, and other revisions. These edits attempt to standardize Medicare payment policies across all of the agency's regional carriers. The CCI edits also identify common instances of "unbundling," which is when a provider files claims for several separate services to a patient who was treated for one condition, illness, or injury. In some cases, a CPT code may have grouped (or bundled) those related services together. Because these bundled codes often provide lower reimbursement to the provider than the services charged separately, such unbundling could be viewed as a fraudulent attempt to gain a higher reimbursement. (See Chapter 2 for more information on external financial audits.)

■ Charge Capturing, Billing, and Collection Systems

The process of capturing (recording) the charge for the service rendered to the patient and then billing and collecting for it might seem straightforward, but it is a highly error-prone process in many practices. Many practices rely on paper forms to capture charges in both the hospital and office settings where the providers encounter patients. This capture process may be based on dictated reports, paper forms, handwritten notes, or data entered into computer software programs. Unfortunately, errors in developing the fee schedule, auditing the capture of charges, or ensuring that efficient billing and collection processes are followed may cause charge entries to be incomplete or sometimes not made at all. Thus, the practice cannot receive the full reimbursement for the services its physicians and other providers have rendered.[30]

Patient Encounter Records

Practices find that a well-designed encounter form, whether it is in paper or electronic form, is an efficient way to help the physician quickly and accurately capture the appropriate procedure and diagnosis codes. Physicians usually complete this form during or immediately after an encounter with a patient. The encounter form is an internal document that should be customized for the practice and include the current procedure and diagnosis codes used most frequently by the physicians.[31] A logical layout of information to check off on the form allows the physician to quickly select CPT-4 and ICD-9 codes, document the level of service, and make brief notes. The form could also list fees for various services. The form can be used as a receipt for the patient, to track physician laboratory orders, and to communicate follow-up appointment recommendations. Most important, the form becomes a document of the encounter that can be used to initiate the billing process. Along with the form, more complete documentation is placed into the patient's chart, either electronically or in writing.

Billing Procedures

Well-documented policies and procedures are considered the primary tools for ensuring an appropriate compliance environment and for measuring, evaluating, and systematically improving business processes.[32] The practice should create formal written policies and procedures to cover all aspects of its billing, collecting, and claims processing functions, from coding and charge entry practices to how claims denials and delinquent payments are handled. To avoid business risk to the practice, implement these policies throughout the practice and routinely monitor them.

Month-End Closing

The process of ending a financial reporting period is called "closing the books." This means that billing staff does not enter any new information for the period, unless it is a correction or restatement of previously gathered data. Discounts, payments, or other adjustments to accounts outstanding received after the applicable month's ledger is closed should be entered in the ledger for the month in which they were actually received.

Electronic Claims Processing

Electronic claims processing is the electronic submission of claims to payers or clearinghouses that reformat the data and retransmit it to the appropriate insurance company or fiscal intermediary. Once an option, electronic submission is now a given in most cases. Beginning in 2005, all claims for services to Medicare beneficiaries have been required to be transmitted to the program in a format that complies with the Health Insurance Portability and Accountability Act (HIPAA) electronic transactions standards. Following the lead of the Medicare program, most private insurance companies also require medical practices to submit claims electronically. Many medical practices dealt with this challenge by upgrading their internal billing systems to submit HIPAA-compliant electronic claims directly to Medicare and payers. Practices that had already invested in a practice management system that could produce electronic claims in compliance with the HIPAA-standard electronic transactions standards are using clearinghouses to translate their claims into the HIPAA-standard formats. Practices that want to continue using paper-based billing are faced with the more expensive and time-consuming process of sending paper claims to a billing service where they are converted into an electronic format. The billing service sends the converted claims to a clearinghouse that translates them to the HIPAA-standard format and then, finally, the claims are sent to payers.

The demand that practices use electronic claims processing by federal payers and, increasingly, private payers is not the only reason to use this technology. Other benefits are that electronic processing allows a practice to:

- Edit (and correct) claims before submitting them to payers;
- Generate productivity reports;

- Reduce rebilling; and
- Improve cost-effectiveness in billing.

Manual Process/Computer System

Small and newly formed medical groups may find that a manual system of receivable record-keeping is an efficient and practical way to maintain patients' transactions. Those practices may feel that their businesses are not yet large enough to justify the purchase of a computer system. Many new practices, even small ones, should view the start-up of a new practice as a prime opportunity to implement an electronic health record (EHR) system that is fully integrated with a computerized practice management system. This up-front commitment will prevent the disruptive and potentially more expensive conversion to EHRs that the practice will eventually have to make – a direction that government policymakers are strongly urging. Even though practices with a relatively high volume of transactions can operate efficiently on a manual system, computerized record-keeping improves the financial manager's ability to control accounts receivable, monitor billings, and ensure collections. This includes taking a systematic and efficient approach to patient billing and effective summary reports to help maintain budgeted cash inflows. An EHR system can also vastly improve the clinicians' abilities to track and monitor the care of patient populations.

Collection Agency Policy

A collection agency can be an important component of an effective collections program for medical practices. Traditionally, medical groups opted to outsource delinquent accounts to professional collectors after a significant period a time, such as 120 or more days. Some physicians, however, still feel that this option produces a negative impression of their business. In recent years, medical practices have moved toward establishing a greater collections capability in-house. This change, it is reasoned, supports the collections process as part of a continuum, rather than something to hand off after a period of failure. Regardless of how the process is handled, a clear policy guiding collections practices helps improve outcomes and avoids the appearance of discriminating against some patients.

Before referring delinquent accounts to an agency for collection, the practice manager should consider whether:

- Agency fees are reasonable compared with internal collection costs;

- The probability of collection is greater using an agency than using internal resources;

- The account is uncollectible, both practically and legally – many payers set time limits on collections of patient balances; and

- Public relations will suffer. Collections efforts, however polite and courteous, may arouse a patient's anger. An agency may have personnel better equipped to handle collections than the medical practice, but any problems an agency causes will hurt the practice's public image.

When selecting a third party to service accounts, the most important element to consider is the financial integrity of the agency, which is best indicated by a long record of ethical dealings with other clients, particularly medical group practices and other health care providers. Additional factors to consider when selecting an agency are:

- Accurate accounting and recording of all funds collected for other medical group clients;

- Prompt remittance of those collections;

- Awareness of public or patient relations;

- Willingness to respond to special requests and provide reports;

- Net recovery rate;

- Understanding of the special nature of medical accounts;

- References – names of other companies, medical institutions, and professional people whom the agency is servicing; and

- Commissions – agencies usually accept accounts for collection on a contingency basis; that is, no collection, no charge. Contingent fee commissions range from 25 to 40 percent.

Accounts previously handled by other agencies, those that require legal action, and accounts transferred to out-of-town agencies may put the fee at a higher percentage.

To monitor how a collection agency handles your accounts, routinely review the following reports:

- Collection agency performance – This report shows the collection agency's current and year-to-date collections and the total amount of possible collection balances pending.

- Aged trial balance by collection agency – This report shows the aging of accounts listed for collection by date of listing.

- Unpaid accounts submitted to collection agency - This report reflects all accounts submitted to a collection agency prior to 90 days and showing no subsequent payment. This time frame is arbitrary; it may be valuable to review several such reports with varying time limits.

Collection Letters

Form letters are not as effective for collecting health care dollars as they were years ago. Statements, letters, and notices generated by a computer must be constructed to provide a payoff. Careful design is important to ensure best results, both in collection and in public relations. Some useful guidelines to follow are:

- Keep collection letters short and to the point;

- Use letters to follow up on small-balance accounts (telephone calls remain more productive when dealing with insurance companies that owe for large account balances); and

- Keep collection notices and statements simple. Include all information regarding the account – date of service, balance, and account number – on the notice and statements. Also include a return envelope. If the group accepts credit cards, be sure to clearly state this payment option.

Telephone Collection

If sending three or four notices by mail to a patient with a delinquent account is not effective, then conduct a follow-up over the telephone. The practice can effectively do this follow-up; however, the staff assigned to this task should be experienced and well trained. An overly aggressive approach will not only produce negative public relations, it could also violate the Fair Debt Collection Practices Act, which is enforced both administratively and judicially. The Federal Trade Commission can treat a violation of the act as an unfair and deceptive practice under the law. Violators are subject to civil penalties in federal and state courts.

If the collection effort is targeted at a payer who may have several outstanding delinquencies, then staff making these calls should receive reports of aged trial balances arranged by guarantor or responsible party. These reports can help in the telephone follow-up effort because all of the payer's delinquent accounts can be referenced in the same call.

Collection Follow-Up

The account collection process for payment of patient balances involves sending multiple statements to patients after both the primary and any secondary insurance companies have paid their portions of the bill. Practices often choose to send a certain number of statements, such as three, and if the account still remains unpaid, follow up by taking additional actions such as making telephone calls and/or sending collection letters. Practices should develop these steps as part of a comprehensive collection follow-up process to ensure that fair and effective collection steps are attempted before turning the account over to a collection agency. To ensure that internal collection efforts are consistent with the practice's overall style and patient satisfaction goals, the practice administrator may wish to:

- Create protocols and a code of ethics for collections;
- Identify and thoroughly train staff who will be assigned to make patient collection calls;

- Consistently follow timelines for sending collections letters and turning over an account to a collection agency;
- Establish payment plan options;
- Advise and seek all patients' signed consent to the practice's written collections policy, preferably when patients make their first visits to the practice;
- Attempt to collect past-due amounts when patients visit the office;
- Remind patients of past-due amounts when they call to schedule appointments;
- Develop and use a charity care policy for patients experiencing hardship; and
- Follow standard industry practices of declaring A/R as "uncollectible" before outsourcing it a collection agency, but continue monitoring those collections efforts.

Disputes

The practice should carefully develop a written protocol for handling billing disputes with patients. This protocol should designate a trained and experienced member of the staff to handle these situations.

Bankruptcy Claims

Practices should be aware of applicable federal and state law concerning whether and how the practice may continue to pursue unpaid amounts after a patient files for personal bankruptcy protection. Practices normally write these amounts off as "uncollectible."

Settlements

After internal and external collections and negotiations for payments fail, some medical practices choose to pursue unpaid accounts, especially ones with large balances. In many states, the amounts owed may fall within the limits of small claims courts; typically, a magistrate hears these cases and there is no jury. If the practice prevails in court, the practice is responsible for collecting the judgment. Once payment is received or the practice is satisfied that it has collected all that is possible, it must file a Creditor's Satisfaction of Judgment, which tells the court that the case is closed. If the practice does not receive payment, it can ask the court to order the debtor to identify his or her assets for possible liquidation. The magistrate can issue a warrant to require the debtor to respond to this inquiry or face imprisonment for failure to respond. However, the debtor cannot be imprisoned for failure to pay the judgment. With a court judgment, it is possible to garnish the patient's wages. This requires his or her employer to pay the county sheriff as much as 25 percent of the individual's paycheck, which the sheriff then forwards to your practice. Physicians should check their state's judicial branch Website for more information.

Time Payments (Budgeted Payments)

An important step to ensure timely collection of receivables is to grant credit to self-pay patients who have a good credit history and fully accept your payment terms. Many practices provide a range of payment terms. The patient agrees to a particular payment plan and the receivables system reports any deviations from the plan. A patient who agrees to pay in 30 days should be considered delinquent after 60 days. Make sure any automated systems can recognize the various payment terms. For example, a patient may not have paid an account in full at the end of 30 days because the agreement was to pay in three installments over three months. Teach staff to handle patients who wish to make special payment arrangements. When possible, attempt to secure the payment arrangement with the responsible party before the service is provided. A receptionist at the front desk or a cashier at the checkout desk who has access to account information can increase collections and reduce later collection problems. The after-service interview could be a last-chance situation. Even if the patient is returning at a future date, this could be the last convenient opportunity to complete records with information not previously collected. Also, it may be the only opportunity to place a bill before the patient and attempt to collect the balance. Tight control and knowledge of charges and payments are crucial to good cash flow.

An additional tool for improving cash flow in medical groups may be to allow a financial institution to carry patient accounts that need monthly payments. Ideally, practices should avoid contract payments on large balances. Collecting these large amounts a little at a time will tie up cash, require more collection follow-up, and will likely be too costly. Since charging interest has never been a viable alternative for health care receivables, alternative methods to handle accounts that would require long-term monthly payments are to accept credit card payments or bank financing.

Write-Offs

There is a temptation to write off an account rather than refer it to a third-party for collection. This approach has three drawbacks. First, word might get around of the medical group's unwillingness to take all possible steps to collect payment. A reputation of this nature can lead to more chronic debtor nonpayment, thus increasing collection costs considerably. Second, this approach is not fair to paying patients. In the long run, someone must pay for those who do not. An indirect result may be increased charges for all patients. In today's environment, holding down costs must be a prime consideration. Third, Medicare regulations require that a practice make a reasonable attempt to collect monies due. Medicare typically defines attempts as reasonable by considering the amount owed vs. the cost to collect. (In other words, a practice isn't required to try to collect if the attempt costs more than the amount to be collected.) If the balance owed is high, and the practice consistently writes such balances off after sending out a few bills and making some calls, the amount owed may have been greater than the cost to collect. Medicare may view this consistent practice of writing off accounts as a standard discount percentage and uniformly reduce the allowances to the practice.

▨ Develop Reconciliation Systems for Third-Party Payments

The practice revenue cycle extends from day of service, through billing patients and insurance companies, to the actual collection of the cash. Ideally, all services would be paid in cash on the day of service. In reality, most practices send a charge ticket to a billing office where the charges are electronically billed to the patient or an insurance company. This process creates an account receivable (A/R) on the practice's books to be collected and reconciled. The collection and reconciliation of payments is the focus of this section.

The practice's accounts receivable are frequently the largest asset on the books. The loss of even a few percent of A/R can add up to large amounts over time. The cost of implementation and maintenance of an effective denial management and audit program will usually more than pay for itself in improved collections.

Payment Policies

Although practice payment policies are generally related to self-pay patients, the implementation of these policies and educating staff on these policies are part of the practice's overall reimbursement procedure. Accounting for bad debt, collection company submission and recoveries, uninsured write-offs, and payment plans all have to be addressed in the practice's payment policies for accurate accounting and evaluating A/R collection efficiency, and all must take antikickback and Stark laws into account in order to remain compliant.

Third-Party Reimbursement

The majority of A/R due to most practices is from insurance companies. For accounting purposes, it is important to differentiate between charges (practice fees), allowables (amount to be collected by contract from the insurance company and patient), and paid amount (what the insurance company and patient pays).

Payer payments come to the practice with an explanation of benefits (EOB). Patient payments are generally in the form of co-payments collected at the time of service and deductibles paid after balance billing the patient. Ideally, the combined insurance and patient payment will equal the allowable, which will equal what the contract says should be paid. It is important that the practice knows what the contractual allowable should be to avoid underpayments.

Contractual allowables are based on each payer's contract and, in some cases, the provider manual or other documents referenced in the contract. Some practices calculate the allowable amount due for their more common services and compare the payer's EOB statement to this list. Other practices have the entire allowable schedule for all services built into their practice system for automated comparisons. This claim-by-claim audit reduces the possibility of underpayment.

Denial Management

Denial management relates to the nonpayment of claims (the practice bill) by insurance companies. The effective management of denials is one of the more complex parts of overall A/R collections, but it is necessary to avoid potentially significant cumulative losses over time. As with most complex problems, it is best to break denial management into small parts.

The first step is to review the EOBs and categorize the reasons for denials given by insurance companies. Examples include "not a benefit," "no referral," "patient not insured," "service not matching age/sex/diagnosis of the patient," "wrong CPT code," and many others. Payers have a long list of codes, and these are usually identified on the EOB. A practice should develop its own list of the most frequently used denial codes so that payer codes can easily be aggregated for statistical purposes. Payers can then be benchmarked against each other to determine trends and patterns.

The practice's denial codes should be broad enough to segregate denials caused by practice coding issues and those that are payer driven. Every effort should be made to identify and correct internal causes of denials. Reducing denials not only improves cash flow, but reduces rework expenses related to claims processing.

Inappropriate payer denials should be managed aggressively. Correcting (if necessary) and resubmitting the denied claim will rectify the majority of problems for most payers. If this does not work, then the next step is to appeal the denial in accordance with the payer's process. The appeal should be tracked and followed until it is resolved. If there are a large number of similar denials from the same payer, senior payer management should address the issue so that the payer's claims processing system is corrected. Before these issues escalate to a major confrontation, make sure the issue is large enough in terms of total dollars to warrant the extra effort.

Finally, the payer/practice contract or state regulations may require payers to meet certain standards on claim reimbursement to avoid paying penalties or interest. Be aware of these requirements and make sure you collect what is due. If the state requires interest to be paid and the payer does not pay it, consider asking the state insurance commissioner for assistance.

Withhold Tracking

Withholds are when the payer retains part of the payment for a period of time, to be returned at a later date if certain payer and provider objectives are met. This mainly applies to capitation payments, but not fee for service. In general, it is not a good contracting policy to let someone else hold the money of the practice with a "promise" to pay at some indefinite time and under indefinite parameters. Unfortunately, the repayment of withholds to practices isn't as common as the collection of withholds by payers.

If withholds cannot be avoided, the practice should track how much has been withheld over the period of time and follow up with requests for payment. Some practices book the withhold due as an account receivable until reconciled. Do your fact checking! It helps to periodically reconcile with the payer how much is in the withhold account so that disputes are avoided at the end of the withhold period. The basis on which the withhold is repaid or not repaid should be examined and audited if necessary.

Profiling Payers

Much has been written about payers profiling or rating physicians based on quality and cost of services. It is recommended that the practice keep track of payer performance. This type of information can be valuable when renegotiating the contract. A payer that creates chaos in the billing office should pay a higher contract rate than the payer who pays accurately and on time.

Variables that should be tracked include claims payment accuracy and timeliness, number and type of denials, resolution of appeals and other problems, and contract negotiations. The list should be comprehensive enough to evaluate a payer's performance fairly against other payers.

Auditing Payments

Managing the individual claim EOBs is only one way to improve collections. Having an internal audit program to supplement EOB processing is another. The goal in auditing the payer is to determine whether or not the practice is being paid correctly and the payer is complying with the terms of the contract.

There are four steps to consider when structuring the auditing process for the practice. They are:

1. Organize your contract files;

2. Identify and monitor key indicators from the contract;

3. Track and document discrepancies; and

4. Prepare to mediate, arbitrate, or litigate.

Step 1. Organize your contract files. To audit payments and terms, contracts must be readily accessible and located in a central place with easy access to those responsible for auditing. Neatly organized contract files separated by the signed agreement, amendments, and correspondence help the auditor when thumbing through hundreds of contract terms and pages. A separate file for each contract is necessary and should be kept locked and in a safe place. Contracts are assets and can pose problems for the providers if they are lost.

Step 2. Identify key indicators to monitor. There are both financial and operational indicators to monitor. It is important to make a list of the key indicators and monitor the same ones for all payers. This creates consistency and standardization in the review process.

One example is for the practice manager to use the power of the practice management system to compare the EOB allowable on a large number of paid claims against the expected contract allowable. If the sum of the EOB allowable for all the claims is far from the expected contractual reimbursement, there is a problem that requires further investigation.

It may not be feasible to audit all the codes paid by each payer, but a reasonable conclusion might be drawn from a sample of codes. For instance, in many primary care practices, a large proportion of total charges may be aggregated in only 20 CPT codes. These are the codes that should be audited for proper payment.

Many practices have moved to electronic claims submission, and some now receive electronic remittances from payers. Having the computer automatically compare the remittance to the expected allowable is a great way to audit payments.

Other operational indicators include: effective date of the current contract, renewal dates (at least 90 days from notice), termination dates, price increase dates, write-offs for noncovered services, timely filing, timely payment, and denials. (Denials include those caused by both the provider and payer with specific denial types. It is critical to have a process in place to track all payer denials until they are resolved.)

Step 3. Track and document discrepancies. This step is critical if you want to justify through data that a trend or problem exists. It is important to identify the clause in the contract that does or does not gain you reimbursement. This will serve to inform the contracting department that wording may need to be revised on the renewal. Reports that summarize auditing problems by category help to communicate not only with the payer, but also with the senior leaders of the practice.

Auditing should be viewed as a program, with monthly and/ or quarterly reports, listing the payer, audit category, dollars recovered, dollars denied, and dollars pending for recovery. Auditing not only improves the practice's bottom line, but also serves to inform contracting of the changes necessary to prevent the likelihood of further occurrences.

When there is a dispute, it is critical to locate that section in the contract that allows the payer to not pay, and to understand it. Identifying this part of the contract helps the practice better address the issue during the next round of negotiations.

Another strength of payer auditing is that it serves to inform contracting of the issues facing back-end business operations so that specifics can be addressed during contract renegotiations. Real experiences allow the contracting team to ask for things that they might not have known to be problematic in the past.

Step 4. Be prepared to mediate, arbitrate, or litigate. Although these steps are never preferred, sometimes they are necessary to reach a resolution. These steps should be applied judiciously; having a good working relationship with the payer is always desirable. Be sure that all efforts to reach a resolution have been exhausted. Additionally, check the wording in the contract to ensure that you have the right to either arbitration or litigation. Both approaches can be time-consuming and costly, so it is important to weigh the costs and benefits of taking such action. When all else fails, a practice may consider terminating the contract.

◢ Summary

For many practices, the accounts receivable are the largest asset. These assets are also the most illusive to manage and collect. The practice should have strong policies and procedures in place to closely track and collect as much as possible. Having even small gaps in the process can be very costly to the practice over the long term.

Chapter 4 **Analyzing and Reporting Financial Performance**

Data is not information. You have to torture it before it tells all it knows.[33]

FINANCIAL ANALYSIS IS ONE OF THE BEST TOOLS for improving financial performance. By conducting financial analysis, practice leaders can determine where to make the operational changes necessary to increase operational efficiency and improve performance. To perform financial analysis effectively, the administrator must understand financial statements and the basis of accounting used in preparing them.

Even an administrator who relies on an accounting department or an outside accounting firm is often the point person in the practice's financial decision-making process. The administrator must explain financial matters to the practice's governing body – the final decision makers – that often consists primarily of physicians without an extensive financial background.

This chapter begins with an overview of basic financial statements. Next, it explains the cash and accrual methods of accounting and the factors influencing the choice of accounting method. Further, it discusses powerful financial analysis tools, including ratio analysis, internal comparisons, and benchmarking. Finally, the chapter concludes with tips for communicating financial information effectively to stakeholders.

◼ The Basic Financial Statements: An Overview

The basic financial statements are the:

- Balance sheet;
- Income statement;
- Statement of changes in equity; and
- Statement of cash flows.

These financial statements may be prepared using the accrual basis of accounting in accordance with generally accepted accounting principles (GAAP) or some other comprehensive basis of accounting (OCBOA), such as the cash or tax basis. (For more information regarding these two methods of accounting, see the discussion immediately following the financial statement section of this chapter.) This chapter includes examples of both cash and accrual financial statements for Blue Mountain Orthopedic Group, P.C. ("Blue Mountain"),[34] a fictitious practice used for only for illustration (resemblance to any existing practice is purely coincidental).

Balance Sheet

The balance sheet tells what the practice owns (its assets), what it owes (its liabilities), and what its net worth or equity (its net claim on assets after subtracting liabilities) is. True to its name, the balance sheet must balance. The balance sheet equation is:

Assets = Liabilities + Equity

A balance sheet lists the assets and liabilities in the order of their liquidity (how quickly they convert to cash). The most liquid assets and liabilities are called current assets and liabilities because they are expected to convert to cash in less than one year. Examples of current assets include cash and accounts receivable (A/R). Examples of current liabilities include accounts payable, payroll withholdings, and current maturities of long-term debt.

Blue Mountain's balance sheets (Exhibits 20 and 21) do not show any investments. If the practice had short-term investments, these would be included with the current assets. Any long-term investments would appear in a separate section between current assets and property and equipment.

A practice's long-term assets usually consist of medical equipment and other property such as computers, office furniture, and leasehold improvements. The balance sheet shows these items in a separate section, along with their cumulative depreciation and net book value.

Other long-term assets are those with an expected life greater than one year, other than investments, property, and equipment. These are the last group in the assets section. Examples include deposits and intangible assets, such as goodwill.

Long-term liabilities appear in a separate section following the current liabilities. These include debts that the practice will pay in one year or more, such as long-term debt, net of current maturities.

The equity section represents the owners' claim on net assets. These amounts are the result of capital contributed by the owners, as well as the undistributed profits of the practice. The accounts in this section will vary depending on the type of entity. For example, corporate entities will show all classes of stock separately at par value beginning with common stock, followed by any contributed capital in excess of par, and retained earnings. Limited liability entities, partnerships, and sole proprietorships generally combine these amounts as members' capital, partners' capital, or proprietor's capital. Although one amount usually appears in these entities' balance sheets for capital, practices should keep detailed subaccounts for each owner.

The retained earnings or owners' capital accounts should include the current year net income, not just the undistributed amounts from prior years. This is true not only for the year-end financial statements, but also for interim statements. The related computation (adding current net income to equity) is shown in the statement of changes in equity and carried to the balance sheet. This is the secret to balancing the balance sheet!

EXHIBIT 20

Accrual Basis Balance Sheet

Blue Mountain Orthopedic Group, P.C.
Balance Sheet
As of December 31, 20X2 and 20X1

Assets	20X2	20X1
Current Assets:		
Cash	$144,000	$86,000
Patient accounts receivable, net of allowance		
for doubtful accounts of $40,000 in 20X2		
and $35,000 in 20X1	800,000	750,000
Prepaid expenses	35,000	25,000
Total current assets	979,000	861,000
Property and equipment, at cost:		
Leasehold improvements	50,000	50,000
Equipment	700,000	550,000
	750,000	600,000
Less: Accumulated Depreciation	285,000	210,000
Property and equipment, net	465,000	390,000
Other Assets:		
Deposits	1,000	1,000
Total Assets	$1,445,000	$1,252,000
Liabilities and Stockholders' Equity		
Current Liabilities:		
Current maturities of long-term debt	$40,000	$25,000
Accounts payable	38,000	35,000
Accrued payroll taxes	125,000	135,000
Accrued retirement plan contribution	115,000	110,000
Total current liabilities	318,000	305,000
Long-Term Liabilities:		
Long-term debt, less current maturities	135,000	85,000
Deferred taxes	326,000	283,000
Total long-term liabilities	461,000	368,000
Total Liabilties	779,000	673,000
Stockholders' Equity:		
Common stock, $1 par, authorized 20,000 shares:		
issued and outstanding 7,000 Shares	7,000	7,000
Contributed capital in excess of par	14,000	14,000
Retained earnings	645,000	558,000
Total stockholders' equity	666,000	579,000
Total Liabilities and Stockholders' Equity	$1,445,000	$1,252,000

EXHIBIT 21

Income Tax Basis Balance Sheet for Cash Basis Taxpayer

Blue Mountain Orthopedic Group, P.C.
Statement of Assets, Liabilities, and Equities – Income Tax Basis
For the Years Ended December 31, 20X2 and 20X1

Assets	20X2	20X1
Current Assets:		
Cash	$144,000	$86,000
Property and equipment, at cost:		
Leasehold improvements	50,000	50,000
Equipment	700,000	550,000
	750,000	600,000
Less: Accumulated Depreciation	435,000	290,000
Property and equipment, net	315,000	310,000
Other Assets:		
Deposits	1,000	1,000
	–	–
Total other assets	1,000	1,000
Total Assets	$460,000	$397,000

Liabilities and Stockholders' Equity	20X2	20X1
Current Liabilities:		
Current maturities of long-term debt	$40,000	$25,000
Accrued payroll taxes	125,000	135,000
Accrued retirement plan contribution	115,000	110,000
Total current liabilities	280,000	270,000
Long-Term Liabilities:		
Long-term debt, less current maturities	135,000	85,000
Total Liabilties	415,000	355,000
Stockholders' Equity:		
Common stock, $1 par, authorized 20,000 shares:		
issued and outstanding 8,000 Shares	7,000	7,000
Contributed capital in excess of par	14,000	14,000
Retained earnings (deficit)	24,000	21,000
Total stockholders' equity	45,000	42,000
Total Liabilities and Stockholders' Equity	$460,000	$397,000

Income Statement

Whereas the balance sheet shows the practice's assets, liabilities, and equity *at a point in time*, the income statement shows the entity's revenue, expenses, and net income *over a period of time*. The basic equation for the income statement is:

Revenues − Expenses = Net Income or Loss

The standard accounting period is one year. Any audit or review by an outside accounting firm would generally be performed on the annual financial statements. Ordinarily, a practice will also prepare interim financial statements on a monthly basis showing current month and year-to-date amounts on the income statement.

Operating revenues, such as fee-for-service income, capitation income, and other medical revenue, such as medical director fees, appear first on the income statement. GAAP requires that any significant amount of capitation revenue be shown separately from fee-for-service income.

The operating expenses appear next. These expenses relate directly to the production of operating revenues. Both GAAP and OCBOA allow an entity to organize, classify, and subclassify these expenses in a useful or customary manner. One method that works well for most medical practices is to divide these expenses into staff salaries and fringe benefits, services and general expenses, purchased services, and provider-related expenses.[35] The presentation of physician salaries on a practice income statement varies. Corporate practices may include these with operating expenses or as a separate item (as is the case with Blue Mountain's financial statements). For partnerships, proprietorships, and limited liability entities, payments to physician-owners are generally considered distributions of profit.

The next section includes income and expenses from sources other than operations; these include investment income, gains or losses on the sale of used medical equipment, and interest expense. Finally, after deducting income taxes, the income statement shows the practice's net income. Blue Mountain's income statement is combined with its statement of equity as discussed below.

Statement of Changes in Equity

This statement shows the activity in the capital accounts during the period and includes changes in both contributed capital and accumulated earnings accounts. Practices whose changes consist only of net earnings and distributions to owners often combine this statement with the income statement, as is the case with our Blue Mountain example. Groups with more complex equity transactions, such as shareholder buy-ins or buyouts, generally report these transactions in a separate statement.

Statement of Cash Flows

The statement of cash flows explains the practice's sources and uses of cash during the year. The three categories are cash provided or used by:

- Operating activities (the practice's normal business activities);

- Investing activities (sales and purchases of investments, including equipment and other fixed assets); and

- Financing activities (transactions involving the practice's debt and equity).

All of the entity's cash transactions fit into one of these three categories.

The statement can present the section on operating activities using either the direct or indirect method. The direct method lists the gross amounts of the various operating cash receipts and disbursements. The indirect method starts with net income, then reconciles this number to cash flow from operations by adding or subtracting changes in the various current asset and liability accounts and non-cash gains and losses, such as depreciation and gains or losses on the sale of fixed assets. Although the Financial Accounting Standards Board (FASB) recommends the direct approach, which is more intuitive, the indirect method (used in Exhibit 22) is typically easier for accountants to prepare and is more popular.[36]

Entities that use an OCBOA, such as the cash or tax method, are not required to prepare a statement of cash flows.

EXHIBIT 22

Statement of Cash Flows

Blue Mountain Orthopedic Group, P.C.
Statement of Cash Flows
As of December 31, 20X2 and 20X1

	20X2	20X1
Cash Flows from Operating Activities:		
Net Income	$87,000	$76,000
Depreciation	75,000	70,000
Deferred taxes	43,000	38,000
Changes in assets and liabilities:		
(Increase) decrease in accounts receivable	(50,000)	(80,000)
(Increase) decrease in prepaid expenses	(10,000)	2,000
Increase (decrease) in accounts payable	3,000	2,000
Increase (decrease) in payroll taxes payable	(10,000)	5,000
Increase (decrease) in retirement contributions payable	5,000	(10,000)
Net cash flows from operating activities	143,000	103,000
Cash Flows from Investing Activities:		
Purchase of leasehold improvements	–	(10,000)
Purchase of equipment	(150,000)	(25,000)
Net cash flows from investing activities	(150,000)	(35,000)
Cash Flows from Financing Activities:		
Repayment of short-term notes payable	–	(45,000)
Net Borrowings (repayment) of long-term debt	65,000	(25,000)
Proceeds from issuance of common stock	–	3,000
Net cash flows from financing activities	65,000	(67,000)
Increase (decrease) in Cash	58,000	1,000
Cash at Beginning of Year	86,000	85,000
Cash at End of Year	$144,000	$86,000

◾ Bases of Accounting: Cash vs. Accrual

Medical practices generally use either the cash or the accrual method of accounting. According to the Medical Group Management Association's (MGMA's) *2006 Cost Survey Based on 2005 Data,* 83.71 percent of participating single-specialty practices and 56.50 percent of participating multispecialty practices use the cash method for tax purposes; 16.29 percent of participating single-specialty and 43.50 percent of participating multispecialty practices use the accrual method for tax reporting purposes.[37]

The accrual method of accounting is consistent with GAAP. Its principles are determined primarily by the FASB, whose pronouncements constitute GAAP. Government-owned practices also should comply with pronouncements of the Governmental Accounting Standards Board. Other authoritative sources of GAAP include publications and pronouncements of the American Institute of Certified Public Accountants (AICPA). Finally, the usual accounting practices of a particular industry, such as the medical practice industry, constitute GAAP for that industry, as long as they do not contradict official authoritative sources.

The AICPA's audit and accounting guide for the health care industry applies to all health care entities, including medical practices. This guide states that health care organizations should prepare their financial statements in accordance with GAAP.[38]

Despite the fact that GAAP is the usual standard for financial reporting, the AICPA recognizes that for some businesses this method is too cumbersome. In certain situations, organizations may use other accounting methods. These other permissible accounting methods are known as "other comprehensive bases of accounting," or OCBOA.[39]

Often practices prepare their financial statements on a basis that is consistent with the income tax regulations for cash basis taxpayers. Accountants prefer calling these "tax basis" or "income tax basis" statements because the cash basis of accounting for income tax filing is better defined than the cash basis for financial reporting.

Both the cash and tax bases are considered OCBOA. Most physician-owned practices meet the criteria for issuing cash or tax basis financial statements.

Revenue and Expense Recognition: The Basic Difference

The basic and most important difference between the cash and accrual methods is the point at which each recognizes revenues and expenses. Accrual basis organizations recognize revenues when they are earned and expenses when they are incurred. Cash basis organizations recognize revenue when the cash is actually or constructively received and expenses when they are actually or constructively paid.

For a medical practice, this means that an accrual basis practice includes medical revenue on its income statement and the net value of any related A/R on its balance sheet at the time the physician sees the patient. A cash basis practice includes the revenue from the visit in its income statement when it receives payment for the services. It never shows the related A/R on its balance sheet.

EXAMPLE:

During March 2008, Dr. Marcus sees a patient. The practice charges $110 for the services, and the patient pays a $20 co-pay at the time of service. The practice then bills the patient's insurance company, which pays $60 in April 2008. The related contractual write-off is $30.

An accrual basis practice would include $80 in revenue on the March income statement with a $60 net receivable on the March 31 balance sheet.

A cash basis practice would include $20 in revenue in March and $60 in revenue in April. The cash basis practice would never include the related A/R on its balance sheet.

An accrual basis practice would include the expenses related to the visit on the income statement during the period in which the service was performed. Any unpaid amount would be reflected as a liability on the practice's balance sheet until it is paid. A cash basis practice would include the related expenses on its income statement during the period in which they are paid. A cash basis practice would not show the related liabilities, such as accounts payable or accrued payroll, on its balance sheet.

EXAMPLE:

During May 2009, Suburban Family Practice, LLC, incurs $450 worth of laundry and linen expense. It pays this bill on June 10, 2009.

An accrual basis practice would include the $450 as an expense on its May 2009 income statement and as a liability (accounts payable) on its May 31 balance sheet.

A cash basis practice would include the $450 expense on its June 2009 income statement. It would never show this amount as a liability on its balance sheet.

Leaving A/R and accounts payable off their balance sheets does *not* relieve cash basis practices of the need to keep detailed accounting records for receivables and payables. They definitely should. Effective management of A/R and accounts payable is crucial for *both* accrual and cash basis practices. The difference is that cash basis practices don't include uncollected or unpaid amounts on their financial statements.

Refer to the sample financial statements in this chapter. Note that the accrual basis balance sheet (Exhibit 20) includes accounts receivable and accounts payable, whereas the tax/cash basis balance sheet (Exhibit 21) does not. The differences in revenues and expenses between the two income statements (Exhibits 23 and 24) reflect the timing differences between when these were earned or incurred and when the cash was received or paid. Exhibit 25 provides a reconciliation of the differences between the two sets of financial statements for the year 20X2.

Cash Basis Exceptions for Recording Liabilities

Although cash basis practices do not generally accrue expenses, a couple of exceptions exist. First, tax laws allow all taxpayers, including cash basis taxpayers, to deduct qualified retirement plan

EXHIBIT 23

Accrual Basis Statements of Income and Retained Earnings

Blue Mountain Orthopedic Group, P.C.
Statement of Income and Retained Earnings
For the Years Ended December 31, 20X2 and 20X1

	20X2	20X1
Revenues		
Net fee-for-service revenue	$6,930,000	$6,275,000
Capitation Revenue	–	–
Other	55,000	50,000
Net Revenue	6,985,000	6,325,000
Operating Expenses:		
Salary and Fringe Benefits:		
Staff salaries	1,200,000	1,100,000
Payroll taxes	100,000	90,000
Employee benefits	300,000	250,000
Total salary and fringe benefits	1,600,000	1,440,000
Services and General Expenses		
Malpractice insurance	170,000	145,000
Provision for bad debts	180,000	175,000
Medical and surgical supplies	178,000	162,000
Depreciation	75,000	70,000
Rent	400,000	375,000
Information technology	100,000	95,000
Other general and administrative	388,000	367,000
Total services and general expense	1,491,000	1,389,000
Total operating expenses	3,091,000	2,829,000
Net revenue after operating expense	3,894,000	3,496,000
Provider-related expenses:		
Physician salaries and benefits	3,750,000	3,370,000
Net income after provider-related expenses	144,000	126,000
Other Income (Expense):		
Interest expense (net)	(12,000)	(8,000)
Net Income before income taxes	132,000	118,000
Provision for income taxes	45,000	42,000
Net income	87,000	76,000
Retained Earnings, Beginning of Year	558,000	482,000
Retained Earnings, End of Year	$645,000	$558,000

EXHIBIT 24
Income Tax Basis Statements of Income and Retained Earnings for a Cash Basis Taxpayer

Blue Mountain Orthopedic Group, P.C.
Statement of Revenues, Expenses, and Retained Earnings – Income Tax Basis
For the Years Ended December 31, 20X2 and 20X1

	20X2	20X1
Revenues:		
Net fee-for-service revenue	$6,700,000	$6,000,000
Capitation Revenue		
Other	55,000	50,000
Net Revenue	6,755,000	6,050,000
Operating Expenses:		
Salary and Fringe Benefits:		
Staff salaries	1,200,000	1,100,000
Payroll taxes	100,000	90,000
Employee benefits	300,000	250,000
Total salary and fringe benefits	1,600,000	1,440,000
Services and General Expenses		
Malpractice insurance	180,000	150,000
Medical and surgical supplies	175,000	155,000
Depreciation	145,000	80,000
Rent	400,000	375,000
Information technology	100,000	95,000
Other general and administrative	388,000	367,000
Total services and general expense	1,388,000	1,222,000
Total operating expenses	2,988,000	2,662,000
Net revenue after operating expenses	3,767,000	3,388,000
Physician salaries and benefits	3,750,000	3,370,000
Net income after physician salaries and benefits	17,000	18,000
Other Income (Expense):		
Interest expense (net)	(12,000)	(8,000)
Net Income before income taxes	5,000	10,000
Provision for income taxes	2,000	4,000
Net income	3,000	6,000
Retained Earnings (deficit), Beginning of Year	21,000	15,000
Retained Earnings (deficit), End of Year	$24,000	$21,000

EXHIBIT 25

Cash-to-Accrual Adjustments 20X2

Blue Mountain Orthopedic Group, P.C.
Cash-to-Accrual Adjustments
For the Year Ended 20X2

Description	Cash	Adjustments Debit	Adjustments Credit	Accrual
Cash	144,000			144,000
Accounts receivable, net	0	A 800,000		800,000
Prepaid expenses	0	D 35,000		35,000
Leasehold improvements	50,000			50,000
Equipment	700,000			700,000
Accumulated depreciation	(435,000)	C 150,000		(285,000)
Deposits	1,000			1,000
				0
Notes payable				0
Current maturities of long-term debt	(40,000)			(40,000)
Accounts payable	0		B 38,000	(38,000)
Payroll taxes payable	(125,000)			(125,000)
Retirement contributions payable	(115,000)			(115,000)
Long-term debt, less current maturities	(135,000)			(135,000)
Deferred income taxes, long-term			F 326,000	(326,000)
Common stock	(7,000)			(7,000)
Contributed capital in excess of par	(14,000)			(14,000)
Beginning Retained Earnings	(21,000)	B 35,000 / F 283,000	A 750,000 / C 80,000 / D 25,000	(558,000)
	3,000			87,000
Net fee-for-service revenue	(6,700,000)		A 50,000 / E 180,000	(6,930,000)
Other	(55,000)			(55,000)
				0
Staff salaries	1,200,000			1,200,000
Payroll taxes	100,000			100,000
Employee benefits	300,000			300,000
Malpractice insurance	180,000		D 10,000	170,000
Provision for bad debts	0	E 180,000		180,000
Medical and surgical supplies	175,000	B 3,000		178,000
Depreciation	145,000		C 70,000	75,000
Rent	400,000			400,000
Information technology	100,000			100,000
Other general and administrative	388,000			388,000
Physician salaries and benefits	3,750,000			3,750,000
Interest expense	12,000			12,000
Provision for income taxes	2,000	F 43,000		45,000
				0
				0
				0
Net Income (Loss)	(3,000)			(87,000)
		1,529,000	1,529,000	

EXHIBIT 25 *(continued)*

Cash-to-Accrual Adjustments 20X2

Explanation of cash/tax basis to accrual adjustments

Item   Explanation

A   To add *net* accounts receivable to the balance sheet. Note that only the current year change in this amount affects current year income. The prior year amount is reflected in the beginning retained earnings difference.

B   To add accounts payable to the balance sheet. Note that only the current year change in this amount affects current year income. The prior year amount is reflected in the beginning retained earnings difference.

C   To adjust for difference in GAAP depreciation and the amount allowed for tax purposes. Note that only the current year difference affects current year income, while prior years' differences affect the beginning retained earnings, and the cumulative difference affects the accumulated depreciation amount.

D   To recognize the portion of unexpired malpractice insurance as an asset. Again, note that only the current year difference affects the income statement, whereas the prior year difference affects beginning retained earnings.

E   To reclassify bad debt expense as an operating expense. For accrual basis financial statements, "net revenue" is net of contractual adjustments and charity care, but not net of bad debt expense. Because cash basis financial statements only report revenue when it is received (and bad debts are, by definition, never received), cash basis financial statements report "net revenue" net of contractual adjustments, charity care, *and* bad debts.

This is a reclassification entry only; it does not affect the "bottom line," except for timing differences in the "real world."

F   To record the provision for deferred taxes. Again, note that only the current year difference affects the income statement, whereas the prior year difference affects beginning retained earnings.

EXAMPLES OF OTHER DIFFERENCES NOT INCLUDED IN THIS EXAMPLE

- Recognition of investment income;
- Capitalization, amortization, and impairment of intangible assets (i.e., goodwill);
- Accrued payroll, including vacation and sick pay;
- Accrual of claims payable and claims payable IBNR (incurred but not received); and
- Deferred revenue (revenue received in advance as a liability).

contributions if they are made by the tax return due date (including extensions). Thus, the expense and liability for retirement plan contributions are generally the same whether the practice is cash or accrual. Second, cash basis practices generally include unpaid payroll withholdings as liabilities on their balance sheets, and many accrue the employer's portion as well.

Depreciation

An accrual basis practice will make adjustments to its financial statements that are required by GAAP. A cash basis practice will usually make modifications to the strict cash basis of accounting that have substantial support, such as capitalizing fixed assets and recording the related depreciation. Tax basis depreciation expense may differ significantly from that reported on the accrual basis. This is because tax rules often allow accelerated depreciation write-offs in the early years of an asset's life, whereas GAAP generally requires a straight-line or a less aggressive accelerated method.

Deferred Taxes

While accrual basis practices must include GAAP depreciation on their financial statements, they often use accelerated methods for tax purposes. This creates a difference (potentially a significant one) between their financial statements and tax return net incomes. This is just one of many possible book-to-tax differences for accrual basis practices. GAAP requires that practices compute income taxes based on their GAAP income without regard to timing differences. The cumulative difference between the two income tax calculations appears on the balance sheet as deferred taxes. This amount may be an asset or a liability, depending on which tax expense is greater.

Other Differences

Many other differences between the bases of accounting exist. Because many cash basis practices report on the tax basis, some of these differences change when the related tax laws change.

Considerations in Selecting Basis of Accounting

The Audit Myth

One pervasive myth holds that certified public accountants can only audit GAAP financial statements. This is *not* true. Statement on Auditing Standards No. 62 allows audits of OCBOA financial statements in certain situations and provides much of the authoritative guidance for reporting on the cash and tax basis.[40] The criteria in this standard would permit many medical practices to have audited cash or tax basis financial statements.

Revenue Determination

Net revenue is the largest item on most practice financial statements. Because of the differences between gross charges and the amount of revenue ultimately collected, the amount of net revenue on an accrual basis practice's income statement is an accounting estimate. The percentage of contractual write-offs and charity care can shift constantly because of changes in payer mix, fee schedules, deductibles, and economic conditions. The AICPA has cautioned that revenue amounts involving accounting estimates are a fraud risk and have instructed auditors to exercise professional skepticism in auditing these amounts, particularly when they are tied to bonuses or other incentive compensation.[41] For example, a significant portion of the well-publicized fraud at HealthSouth was perpetrated by misstating contractual adjustments.[42] An accrual basis practice must devote the time and other resources necessary to ensure that these computations are reasonably accurate.

Taxes

Most physician-owned practices qualify to use the cash method for income tax purposes. This method usually saves or defers a significant amount of income taxes because the deferral of income tax on A/R is generally much larger than the deductions lost by not being able to deduct accounts payable and other accrued liabilities. Because Section 446(a) of the Internal Revenue Code requires that a taxpayer compute taxable income on the same basis of accounting it regularly uses in keeping its books, these practices must also issue their external financial statements on the cash basis. Although a cash basis practice might prepare internal analyses that include accrual basis attributes for internal management purposes, it should ensure that the financial statements given to third parties, such as bankers, reflect the basis of accounting used in preparing its income tax returns.

Simplicity vs. Economic Reality

Many smaller practices and physician-owned practices that can use the cash method for tax purposes do so because it is easier than the accrual method. Conformity with GAAP involves more than merely adding A/R and accounts payable to the balance sheet. A practice could devote significant resources to computing deferred taxes, accrued vacation pay, the provision for bad debts, and other accrual items.

All these GAAP complexities not only increase the amount of time and other resources required to generate practice financial statements, but they also often make the financial statements more difficult for individuals without a financial background, including many physician-owners, to understand.

Although cash basis financial statements may be easier for physician-owners to understand, they may not reflect economic reality. When accrual basis accounting records transactions are incurred, they result in matching revenues with the related expenses. Because the cash basis records these items when the cash changes hands, such matching is not guaranteed and the financial statements could be badly distorted, particularly for practices with more complex financial situations, such as capitation arrangements with operating liabilities for payments to other providers.

◼ Analytical Procedures

Consultants and outside accountants generate many of their suggestions for clients on how to improve their business operations by applying analytical procedures to financial data. Administrators can use the same procedures to determine operational improvements necessary to improve their practices' performance.

Examples of analytical procedures include:

- Internal comparisons;
- Ratio analysis; and
- Benchmarking financial data against industry data.

Internal comparisons

One good way to begin a financial analysis is by reviewing and comparing the practice's internal data. Useful comparisons include:

- Current data vs. prior period data;
- Current actual data vs. budgets, forecasts, or other prospective data; and
- By business segment, such as department, location, or specialty.

Current Data vs. Prior Period Data

One popular analysis method is to compare current year amounts against equivalent prior year amounts, including variances in terms of both the dollar amount and as a percentage of the prior period balance, and investigating significant variances. This analysis is usually more meaningful when performed on income statement rather than balance sheet amounts. Generally, income statement numbers are more stable because they represent a period of time, whereas the balance sheet shows amounts at a point in time. Exhibit 26 shows this comparison for Blue Mountain Orthopedic Group, P.C.

Some popular accounting packages have report writer modules that can generate this report. Outside accountants who prepare practice financial statements may also be able to generate these reports through their client accounting software.

Current Actual Data vs. Budgets, Forecasts, or Other Prospective Data

Practice administrators can use the same format as that shown in Exhibit 26 to compute differences between the current period actual numbers and those contained in budgets, forecasts, or other prospective analyses.

EXHIBIT 26
Internal Comparisons of Income Statement Data for Current vs. Prior Year

Blue Mountain Orthopedic Group, P.C.
Analytical Review of Income Statement Data
For the Years Ended 20X2 vs. 20X1

	20X2	%	20X1	%	Net Change	%
Revenues:						
Net fee-for-service revenue	$6,930,000	99.21%	$6,275,000	99.21%	$655,000	10.44%
Capitation Revenue	–	0.00%	–	0.00%	–	
Other	55,000	0.79%	50,000	0.79%	5,000	10.00%
Net Revenue	6,985,000	100.00%	6,325,000	100.00%	660,000	10.43%
Operating Expenses:						
Salary and Fringe Benefits:						
Staff salaries	1,200,000	17.18%	1,100,000	17.39%	100,000	9.09%
Payroll taxes	100,000	1.43%	90,000	1.42%	10,000	11.11%
Employee benefits	300,000	4.29%	250,000	3.95%	50,000	20.00%
Total salary and fringe benefits	1,600,000	22.91%	1,440,000	22.77%	160,000	11.11%
Services and General Expenses						
Malpractice insurance	170,000	2.43%	145,000	2.29%	25,000	17.24%
Provision for bad debts	180,000	2.58%	175,000	2.77%	5,000	2.86%
Medical and surgical supplies	178,000	2.55%	162,000	2.56%	16,000	9.88%
Depreciation	75,000	1.07%	70,000	1.11%	5,000	7.14%
Rent	400,000	5.73%	375,000	5.93%	25,000	6.67%
Information technology	100,000	1.43%	95,000	1.50%	5,000	5.26%
Other general and administrative	388,000	5.55%	367,000	5.80%	21,000	5.72%
Total services and general expense	1,491,000	21.35%	1,389,000	21.96%	102,000	7.34%
Total operating expenses	3,091,000	44.25%	2,829,000	44.73%	262,000	9.26%
Net revenue after operating expenses	3,894,000	55.75%	3,496,000	55.27%	398,000	11.38%
Provider-related expenses:						
Physician salaries and benefits	3,750,000	53.69%	3,370,000	53.28%	380,000	11.28%
Net income after provider-related expense	144,000	2.06%	126,000	1.99%	18,000	14.29%
Other Income (Expense):						
Interest expense (net)	(12,000)	-0.17%	(8,000)	-0.13%	(4,000)	50.00%
Net income before income taxes	132,000	1.89%	118,000	1.87%	14,000	11.86%
Provision for income taxes	45,000	0.64%	42,000	0.66%	3,000	7.14%
Net income	87,000	1.25%	76,000	1.20%	11,000	14.47%
Retained Earnings, Beginning of Year	558,000	7.99%	482,000	7.62%	76,000	15.77%
Retained Earnings, End of Year	$645,000	9.23%	$558,000	8.82%	$87,000	15.59%

By Business Segment

Comparing financial data among business segments such as practice locations, specialties, or other divisions is a useful technique for discovering inefficiencies, underperformers, best practices, and accounting errors. These comparisons can be done using actual amounts, but they are often more meaningful when comparing ratios, such as the ones discussed in the next section.

Ratio Analysis and Comparisons with Nonfinancial Data

Ratio analysis is the study of relationships between financial statement amounts. Similar computations involve relationships between financial and nonfinancial data. Ratios are particularly useful when they involve data that have a stable relationship.

Ratios usually result in more meaningful comparisons against outside data than raw dollar amounts, and are also better for some internal comparisons. This section highlights some of the more useful ratios and comparisons for medical practices. The typical range of these ratios will vary by specialty and the attributes of the particular practice.

Balance Sheet

Traditional balance sheet ratios may not be meaningful for many medical practices. Physician-owned practices often pay all or most of their profits as bonuses or other distributions to the physicians, and thus may not have a large amount of equity. Practices on the cash basis of accounting do not include key balance sheet amounts for A/R and accounts payable on their balance sheet.

Current ratio. This liquidity ratio measures the practice's ability to meet its immediate financial obligations. Bankers use this ratio in assessing credit risk.

Current Assets ÷ Current Liabilities
20X2: $979,000 ÷ $318,000 = 3.08
20X1: $861,000 ÷ $305,000= 2.82

Debt-equity ratio. This ratio measures the practice's leverage. Bankers generally consider lower ratios (less debt) better.

$$\text{Total Liabilities} \div \text{Total Liabilities and Stockholders' Equity}$$
$$\text{20X2: } \$779,000 \div \$1,445,000 = 0.54$$
$$\text{20X1: } \$673,000 \div \$1,252,000 = 0.54$$

Revenue Cycle

Net revenue is usually the largest item on a practice's financial statements, and revenue cycle ratios are popular. Additionally, many of the ratios involving operating expenses and profitability analyze these amounts based on their relationship to net revenue.

Net revenue per full-time-equivalent physician. Because Blue Mountain has seven FTE physicians, that group would compute this ratio as follows:

$$\text{Net Revenue} \div \text{Number of FTE Physicians}$$
$$\text{20X2: } \$6,985,000 \div 7 = \$997,857$$
$$\text{20X1: } \$6,325,000 \div 7 = \$903,571$$

Gross collection ratio. This ratio computes net collections as a percentage of gross charges; it can be useful for predicting future cash receipts and assessing the overall reasonableness of the practice's fee schedule. It may also be helpful in payer contract negotiations and assessing contract profitability.

This ratio varies among specialties and even between practices within a certain specialty. For example, the MGMA *Cost Survey for Single-Specialty Practices 2008 Report Based on 2007 Data* reports median gross fee-for-service collections of 65.90 percent for pediatrics; with 58.92 percent at the 25th percentile and 72.55 percent at the 75th percentile.[43] Comparable statistics for cardiology are median gross fee-for-service collections of 35.42 percent, with 31.26 percent at the 25th percentile and 50.37 percent at the 75th percentile.[44]

Because fee schedules vary significantly among practices and a practice may change its fee schedule philosophy over time, this ratio is usually not meaningful in assessing billing and collection performance.

Net Collections ÷ Gross Charges
20X2: $6,700,000 ÷ $12,000,000 = 55.83%
20X1: $6,000,000 ÷ $11,000,000 = 54.54%

Adjusted (or net) collection ratio. This ratio gives the amount actually collected as a percentage of what was theoretically collectible. The denominator subtracts contractual adjustments and charity care, but not bad debts and other write-offs, from gross collections in determining the amount theoretically collectible.

This ratio is an important indicator in assessing billing and collection performance.

Net Collections ÷ (Gross Charges − Contractual Write-Offs − Charity Care)
20X2: $6,700,000 ÷ ($12,000,000 − 4,820,000 − 270,000) = 96.96%
20X1: $6,000,000 ÷ ($11,000,000 − 4,450,000 − 260,000) = 95.39%

According to data in the MGMA *Cost Survey for Single-Specialty Practices 2008 Report Based on 2007 Data*, this ratio varies somewhat among specialties and is usually between 95 percent and 100 percent. For example, adjusted collection rates were 97.41 percent for ophthalmology, 100.00 percent for urology, and 94.59 percent for general surgery.[45]

Days in A/R. This ratio, which gives the number of days' charges the practice has in A/R, indicates how quickly the practice collects its fees or resolves its charges. It is an important indicator in assessing billing and collection performance.

Gross Accounts Receivable ÷ (Annual Gross Charges ÷ 365)
20X2: $1,350,000 ÷ ($12,000,000 ÷ 365) = 41.06
20X1: $ 1,280,000 ÷ ($11,000,000 ÷ 365) = 42.47

This metric varies somewhat among specialties. For example, according the MGMA *Cost Survey for Single-Specialty Practices 2008 Report Based on 2007 Data,* radiology (46.95 days) and anesthesiology (48.14%) had some of the highest median days in A/R. These are hospital-based specialties that do not usually have an opportunity to collect from patients at the time of service. Practices who traditionally see more patients in their office had some of the lower median days in A/R. For example, the reported median days in A/R were 27.96 for internal medicine and 32.33 for ophthalmology.[46]

A/R aging. In computing this ratio, the practice computes the percentage of its A/R in certain aging categories as a percentage of total A/R. Categories frequently compared are the percentages of more than 90 days and those more than 120 days.

Like the days in the A/R ratio, this computation indicates how quickly the practice collects or resolves its charges and is an important indicator of billing and collection performance. Analyzing the A/R aging by payer can help identify collection problems.

Age (days)	Percentage	Amount
0–30	59.00	$796,500
31–60	15.00	202,500
61–90	9.00	121,500
90–120	4.00	54,000
120+	13.00	175,500
Total	100.0	$1,350,000

Payroll/Staffing

Because payroll is the largest expense for most medical practices, staffing ratios are important for analyzing practice operations. For the purposes of the staffing ratio, payroll costs exclude physician costs such as salaries, bonuses, payroll taxes, retirement plan contributions, insurance, and other benefits. These ratios can include or exclude nonphysician provider costs in the numerator. Understanding whether nonphysician providers are included in payroll costs is important when benchmarking this ratio against industry data.

Payroll ratio. This ratio expresses payroll costs as a percentage of net revenue.

Nonprovider Payroll Costs ÷ Net Revenue
20X2: $1,600,000 ÷ 6,985,000 = 22.91%
20X1: $1,440,000 ÷ 6,325,000 = 22.77%

Payroll cost per FTE physician. This ratio expresses the dollar amount of staffing cost per FTE physician.

Nonprovider Payroll Costs ÷ FTE Physicians
20X2: $1,600,000 ÷ 7 = $228,571
20X1: $1,440,000 ÷ 7 = $205,714

Payroll cost varies by specialty. For example, recent MGMA cost survey data report median support staff cost for multispecialty practices of 30.30 percent[47] compared with that for single-specialty radiology practices of 12.35 percent.[48]

Employee turnover ratio. Although turnover data come from personnel records rather than financial statements, this ratio is significant because turnover often has an adverse effect on profitability and operations. Thus, a high turnover ratio (20 percent or greater) usually indicates room for improvement.

Total FTEs who have left the practice during the year ÷ total FTEs employed by the practice:

EXAMPLE
10/50 = 20% Turnover

Lower payroll and overhead costs are not necessarily better. Although a practice improves profitability by eliminating unnecessary or inefficient costs, expenditures in the right places allow the physicians – the primary revenue generators – to be more efficient, thus enabling the practice to earn more revenue. When a practice cuts the wrong overhead costs, revenue and profitability suffer.

Overhead (Operating Cost)

For the purposes of this ratio, overhead means all operating expenses, including staff payroll but excluding provider or physician costs. As with the payroll ratios, it is important to understand whether nonphysician provider costs are included in benchmarking data. Similar ratios may be computed on individual overhead line items, such as medical and surgical supplies, or groups of related overhead expenses, such as billing costs.

Overhead ratio. This ratio expresses overhead as a percentage of net revenue.

Operating Costs ÷ Net Revenue
20X2: $3,091,000 ÷ $6,985,000 = 44.25%
20X1: $2,829,000 ÷ $6,325,000 = 44.73%

This and similar ratios vary significantly among specialties. For example, the MGMA *Cost Survey for Single-Specialty Practices 2008 Report Based on 2007 Data* reports median operating cost as a percentage of total medical revenue of 61.74 percent for ophthalmology and 27.45 percent for radiology.[49]

Overhead per FTE physician. This ratio expresses the dollar amount of overhead per FTE physician.

Overhead Costs ÷ FTE Physicians
20X2: $3,091,000 ÷ 7 = $441,571
20X1: $2,829,000 ÷7 = $404,143

Medical and surgical supplies ratio. This is an example of the ratio of a particular line item cost to net revenue.

Medical and Surgical Supplies Costs ÷ Net Revenue
20X2: $178,000 ÷ $6,985,000 = 2.55%
20X1: $162,000 ÷ $6,325,000 = 2.56%

Medical and surgical supplies per FTE physician. This is an example of computing the dollar value of an individual overhead line item per FTE physician.

Medical and Surgical Supplies Costs ÷ FTE Physicians
20X2: $178,000 ÷ 7 = $25,429
20X1: $162,000 ÷ 7 = $23,143

Because the medical and surgical supplies expense tends to vary directly with volume, the medical and surgical supplies ratio would usually be more meaningful than the cost per FTE physician in identifying a group's potential for savings in this area. Because this percentage varies somewhat among specialties, comparisons against same specialty data are most meaningful.

Profitability

Although other ratios are important because they affect the bottom line, profitability *is* the bottom line. When computing medical practice profitability for physician-owned practices, the focus is on the amount of money available for distribution to the physicians, which usually differs from net income. This difference may be large or small, depending on the type of entity, the basis of accounting, and other practice attributes.

One common indicator involves the "total medical revenue after operating costs." For the purposes of this computation, operating costs do not include physician compensation or benefits. (Note: Because income statement presentation of physician compensation varies among practices, a prerequisite to properly computing this amount is understanding how this information is presented in the practice's financial statements.)

Two advantages of using this amount in profitability ratios are (1) comparative MGMA cost survey data are available for many specialties, and (2) they enable comparisons between practices with different legal entity structures. For example, corporate practices report salary expenses for their physicians, while limited liability entities, partnerships, and proprietorships compensate their physician-owners primarily through distribution of practice net income. Because this metric is based on revenues and expenses prior to payments to physicians, the amounts are analogous.

Total medical revenue after operating costs as a percentage of net revenue. This percentage will vary among specialties. For example, hospital-based specialties (anesthesiology, pathology, and radiology) and surgical specialties generally have higher percentages than internal medicine and other specialties in which physicians have a large volume of office visits (and correspondingly higher staffing and other overhead costs).

Total Medical Revenue After Operating Costs ÷ Net Revenues
20X2: $3,894,000 ÷ $6,985,000 = 55.74%
20X1: $3,496,000 ÷ $6,325,000 = 55.27%

Total medical revenue after operating costs per FTE physician. This is arguably the best indicator of practice performance. Although practices have different cost structures and revenue levels, this ratio reveals how well these attributes come together to create profit.

Total Medical Revenue After Operating Costs ÷ FTE Physicians
20X2: $3,894,000 ÷ 7 = $556,286
20X1: $3,496,000 ÷ 7 = $499,429

Profitability indicators vary significantly among the various specialties. For example, the MGMA *Cost Survey for Single-Specialty Practices 2008 Report Based on 2007 Data* reports median total medical revenue after operating and nonphysician provider costs per FTE physician of $643,871 for orthopedic surgery, $568,803 for urology, and $491,402 for pediatrics.[50]

Benchmarking

Webster's New Collegiate Dictionary defines benchmarking as "a standard by which something can be measured or judged."[51] The Xerox Corporation says that benchmarking is "the continuous process of measuring products, services and practices against the toughest competitors or those companies recognized as industry leaders (best in class)."[52]

Our society benchmarks many activities, ranging from business and industry to leisure pursuits. Automobile manufacturers benchmark miles per gallon and annual fuel costs; these data are required to be displayed on new car window stickers. Major appliance manufacturers must post energy efficiency ratings on all appliances to compare energy usage against similar appliances. Sports benchmarks include batting averages for baseball players and efficiency ratings for football quarterbacks.

Benchmarking has come to health care in reports of top hospitals, managed care premium networks, and, more recently, pay for performance.

For medical practices, benchmarking is another financial analysis tool for improving performance. Medical groups can apply the benchmarking process both internally and externally to identify opportunities for operational improvement.

The major benefits of benchmarking for medical practices include the following:

- It allows the practice to measure its performance;
- It quantifies the practice's performance relative to others;
- It identifies opportunities for improvement;
- It generates new ideas and creative thinking;
- It provides a basis for strategic planning;
- It is an objective, data-driven process that is generally accepted by physicians; and
- It encourages teamwork and collaboration.

Benchmarking does have limitations; among the major ones are the following:

- One benchmark is not enough;
- Practices must benchmark results and processes;
- Benchmarking requires time and thought;
- Comparison data are never perfect;
- Comparison data may not be timely;
- Benchmarking requires open, honest, and objective assessments; and
- It requires the mutual sharing of benchmarking information.

MGMA provides external benchmarking information to medical practices through many of its products and services. Its annual *Physician Compensation and Production Surveys*, annual *Cost Surveys*, and *Performances and Practices of Successful Medical Groups* provide comparative statistical data regarding medical practice performance. Other MGMA resources include information exchanges, e-mail forms, inquiries, and networking opportunities. Many other organizations also provide relevant external benchmarking information; these include the American Medical Association, the American Medical Group Association, the Association of American Medical Colleges, and a number of physician specialty societies.

Before attempting to create benchmarks, it is important to understand the benchmarking process. A practice must be selective about what it attempts to benchmark, and it must benchmark those areas that can be changed by management. The customary steps in the benchmarking process are:

1. Identify the areas of the practice to be reviewed and improved;

2. Understand the practice's current process or information;

3. Determine specific processes or results to be benchmarked;

4. Identify peer groups and source information;

5. Collect and compile accurate data;

6. Analyze results;

7. Make recommendations for improvement;

8. Implement recommendations; and

9. Measure and report the results;

Most medical practices benchmark data internally, externally, or both. Internal benchmarking includes physician-to-physician benchmarking, office-to-office benchmarking, and service-line-to-service-line benchmarking.

In external benchmarking, the practice compares physician productivity and clinical quality to external clinical benchmarks and financial results to external benchmarks in business areas. Included in the appendixes to this chapter are examples of benchmarking for the fictitious practice Deep South Obstetrics and Gynecology,

P.C. (any resemblance to an actual practice is purely coincidental).[53] These are:

- Appendix 3.1, Benchmark Against MGMA Cost Survey Overall per FTE Physician;

- Appendix 3.2, Benchmark Against MGMA Cost Survey Overall Percentage of Total Medical Revenue;

- Appendix 3.3, Benchmark Against MGMA Cost Survey Staffing per FTE Physician; and

- Appendix 3.4, Benchmark Against MGMA with Compensation.

A careful review of areas in which the practice is significantly over or under the benchmark will identify areas that are functioning very well and those that need improvement.

Presenting Financial Information to Physicians and Other Stakeholders

Although the administrator frequently performs much of the practice's financial analysis, physicians and other stakeholders often have the ultimate responsibility for practice activities and major financial decisions. For example, the governing body anticipates cash flow and assesses management's performance. It makes crucial decisions on whether to add another physician, buy a building, offer ancillary services, and many other issues.

To fulfill these responsibilities, decision makers need timely and relevant information on the practice's financial performance. On some occasions, they may need special analyses such as the return-on-investment computations. The administrator must ensure that these stakeholders not only receive this information, but that they understand it well enough to make informed decisions. This task can be especially challenging when some decision makers have limited financial knowledge. At the same time, however, the administrator must present enough financial detail to those stakeholders who are financially astute.

Providing Information

The administrator should provide agreed-upon financial reports to physicians and other stakeholders on a regular basis. These normally include financial statements, budget comparisons, billing information, and clinical productivity. Depending on the nature of the practice, stakeholders may want other reports, such as referring physician analyses or appointment availability. Providing a dashboard of summary financial data, including some of the ratios discussed in this chapter, gives an executive summary of practice performance.

Some of the most important reporting projects are those special reports that the administrator prepares on an as-needed basis to facilitate a particular decision, such as whether to invest in an electronic health record system or whether to change the way the group's employee health insurance is handled.

Explaining Financial Information

Whereas financially astute administrators may take pride in their detailed financial analyses, these analyses may confuse some stakeholders. This section discusses tools and techniques that administrators have used successfully to communicate financial information to their governing bodies. The success of a particular method will vary depending on the attributes of the situation, the practice, the administrator, and the individual stakeholders.

Using Words to Explain Numbers

Administrators have reported success using both written and oral communication to explain financial data to stakeholders.

Letters and memos from management. Providing a management letter with the regular financial reports offers an interpretation of the numbers and insight into what is happening in the practice. Consider the following example:

> As you can see, the total charges and the number of procedures are up for the year-to-date compared to last year. These increases are primarily a result of increased patient volume at the East Side Clinic.

Unfortunately, collections for August were lower than expected. This occurred because we had difficulty getting paid by ABC Healthcare. Evidently this payer's recent computer update resulted in a "bug" in its system that mistakenly rejected our claims as noncovered services. ABC was able to fix the bug, and we received these payments in early September....

Oral presentations. The administrator will often have to explain financial information at board meetings. Good presentation skills, including the ability to discuss complex financial matters in common terms, are essential.

One-on-one discussions. These can be useful with stakeholders of all levels of financial knowledge. The administrator can explain financial basics to those without financial backgrounds. This gives nonexpert stakeholders an opportunity to ask questions – something they may be hesitant to do in a larger group.

For financially astute shareholders, one-on-one discussions can provide a venue for in-depth discussions of financial issues, complete with technical language. Physicians with the stronger financial backgrounds can often help explain these issues to other physicians.

Bars and Graphs

Seeing is believing. Converting technical financial data to pie charts, graphs, and bar charts creates something all members of the group can understand. Inserting one or more of these graphics into a memo or management report makes the message clearer.

Technology

Today's technology provides options beyond the paper report for distributing financial information. Administrators can e-mail the files or put the information on a CD or DVD. A Web portal can provide online access to prepared reports or real-time access to financial data. These portals allow stakeholders to select the amount of detail they wish to view. Some may review the dashboard and various bars and graphs, whereas others may study the detailed data in the supporting spreadsheets.

▨ Summary

Through financial analysis, medical practices can discover many ways to improve their operations and productivity. Popular forms of this analyses for medical practices include internal comparisons, ratio analyses, and benchmarking. These methods provide tools for assessing the practice's revenue cycle, staffing, overhead, general profitability, and creditworthiness.

Understanding financial statements and the related basis of accounting are prerequisites to performing sound financial analysis. But understanding financial matters is not just for the administrator and financial staff; the members of the governing body have the ultimate responsibility for making important financial decisions. Many stakeholders may not have an extensive financial background, and therefore they rely on the administrator and other financial personnel to explain the pertinent information to them. Consequently, practice administrators not only need to have a thorough working knowledge of these matters, but they also must be able to communicate them effectively to members of the governing body.

Chapter 5 **Directing Banking, Investment, and Other Financial Relationships**

Increasingly, a useful expert is not someone with (containing) all the answers, but someone who knows where to find answers. The new experts have value ... by being great "pointers" to other people and to useful, current information.[54]

WHILE PRACTICE ADMINISTRATORS NEED TO POSSESS a broad understanding of the various components of financial management, they cannot do it all or know it all. The ability to select and use competent financial advisors is often vital to an administrator's effectiveness. Medical practices commonly use outside accountants, bankers, attorneys, investment advisors, retirement plan administrators, and consultants. The extent to which a practice draws on these outside advisors depends on the knowledge and skills of internal personnel, the nature of the desired services, the size of the practice, and other practice attributes.

In choosing an advisor, look for one with a good reputation, appropriate credentials, and experience working with medical practices. References from other physician groups are often useful. Don't overlook the potential for referrals from the practice's existing advisors. For example, an attorney may be able to recommend a good accountant; an accountant may be able to recommend a good banker or investment advisor. Be aware, however, that some overlap exists among the services that the various advisors perform. For example, banks and insurance agents often provide investment advisory services. Accountants and banks may also provide retirement plan administration.

The comfort level and ease with which the physicians, administrator, and other members of the management team communicate with these advisors is crucial to their effectiveness. In addition, outside advisors must often communicate with each other. Credentialed advisors provide little benefit if practice leaders do not understand their advice or do not receive it in a timely manner. For example, the practice may owe unanticipated income taxes if the accountant and practice administrator cannot work together to project income, depreciation, retirement contributions, and cash flow in connection with year-end tax planning.

Keep in mind that character counts. An advisor may need to help the group deal with difficult or controversial issues, such as restructuring the physician compensation plan or testifying in court regarding practice financial matters in the event of an owner's divorce.

Avoid potential conflicts of interest. Before engaging a physician's family member or close friend, consider whether all members of the leadership group trust this potential advisor to be impartial in helping resolve disputes or problematic situations within the practice.

Accountants

One of the most important advisors is the outside accountant. The certified public accountant (CPA) has passed a four-part, two-and-a-half-day exam demonstrating competence in accounting practice, theory, auditing, and business law. CPAs must complete continuing professional education to maintain their licenses. Although education requirements vary by state, to take the CPA exam an accountant must generally have at least an undergraduate degree with a specified minimum amount of accounting and business courses.

Accountants may practice alone or as part of a firm. Some practices prefer to use an individual practitioner or a small firm because they believe they will receive more individual attention. Larger firms usually provide a wider range of services.

Ensure that the practice receives an engagement letter. This letter, written by the accounting firm, delineates the services the firm will perform, what work products the firm will deliver, and when and how it will charge for these services. It will also contain standard language and disclaimers regarding the accountant's services. Don't be alarmed by this language – the American Institute of Certified Public Accountants (AICPA) recommends that accountants use it.

Accounting and Auditing Services

These are, perhaps, the services most frequently associated with accountants. An outside accountant may provide three levels of services with respect to financial statements. Audits are the highest, reviews are the middle, and compilations are the lowest level of service and cost. With each of these engagements, the accountant will issue a report, but the nature of the report and the accountant's responsibility will vary according to the level of service.

Audits

An audit is the only level of service in which the accountant renders an opinion on the financial statements. The audit report indicates whether the financial statements fairly present the financial condition and results of operations for the practice in accordance with generally accepted accounting principles (GAAP) or some other comprehensive basis of accounting (OCBOA), such as the tax or cash basis. In the event that the accountants cannot obtain enough information to issue an opinion, they will issue a disclaimer. (See a comparison of the different types of audit reports in Exhibit 27.)

In performing an audit, the accountant obtains outside corroborative evidence, assesses internal control and the related risks, and performs inquiries and analytical procedures. The auditor must also obtain written representations signed by responsible management personnel, such as the administrator, physician leader, and/or financial officer, regarding the financial statements.

Clarification: Financial statement audits vs. other types of audits. A practice may have several types of audits. The audit described above is an audit of the financial statements in accordance with generally accepted auditing standards. Governmental tax authorities such as the Internal Revenue Service or state department of revenue might audit the practice's tax returns – and possibly audit its owners' individual returns in connection with that audit. A practice may engage a consultant or accounting firm to conduct a billing audit or an operational audit. Finally, the Office of Inspector General or other governmental payer may audit a practice's billing records if it suspects billing fraud.

Searching for fraud is *not* the primary purpose of an audit of the financial statements. Auditors attempt to obtain sufficient evidence to provide reasonable assurance that the financial statements are free from material misstatements, *including* material misstatements

---

EXHIBIT 27

Types of Audit Reports

Type of Opinion	Explanation
Unqualified	The most desirable: Reasonable assurance that the financial statements are fairly presented in accordance with GAAP or OCBOA.
Qualified	The financial statements are generally in accordance with GAAP or OCBOA, but the auditor has a reservation about a financial statement matter that prevents him or her from issuing an unqualified opinion. The accountant's report describes this issue.
Adverse	The financial statements contain material discrepancies from GAAP or OCBOA. The accountant's report explains the matter.
Disclaimer	The auditor cannot obtain sufficient information to issue an opinion.

created by fraud. In response to some of the more recent accounting scandals, the Auditing Standards Board and the AICPA have released guidance to auditors to help ensure that they discover frauds that create material financial misstatements.[55]

Reviews

A review is substantially less involved in scope than an audit. The objective of a review is for the accountant to provide *limited assurance* regarding the financial statements. In performing a review, the accountant primarily focuses on inquiries and analytical procedures. As in an audit, the accountant requests that practice leaders sign management representation letters. A review differs from an audit in that the accountant does not usually obtain outside corroborative evidence or assess internal control and the related risks.[56]

Compilations

A compilation is the lowest level of service that an independent CPA may perform with respect to financial statements. The objective of a compilation is for the accountant to present, in the form of financial statements, information that is representative of management. In performing a compilation, the accountant provides no opinion on the financial statements and no assurance that the statements are fairly presented. The accountant is only required to read the financial statements and consider whether they are appropriate in form and free from material errors.[57]

Obviously, many accountants who issue compilation reports have done much more with their clients' financial statements than simply read them. Accounting standards require that accountants make inquiries or perform additional procedures if they become aware of or suspect that the financial statements could be incomplete, incorrect, or misleading. In addition, for medical practices that are usually smaller, accounting firms often maintain the general ledger and issue compilation reports on the related computerized interim and annual financial statements.

Considerations in Selecting Level of Service

Although an audit provides the most assurance, it is usually much more expensive than a review or compilation. Many practices that have an audit do so because their creditors, investors, or a regulatory body require it.

The middle level of service, the review, generally costs less than an audit but more than a compilation. Although a review does not provide the level of assurance that an audit does, the fact that the outside accountant performs inquiries and analytical procedures is an important consideration. A study of some of the more notorious accounting scandals concluded that these frauds would have been discovered sooner had the auditors done a better job of using simple analytical procedures.[58] The review may be an appropriate level of service for a practice that prepares its financial statements internally, but is not required to have an audit. It provides a check on practice financial reports, but at a lower cost.

A compilation is usually the least expensive level of service. Although a compilation provides no assurance on the financial statements, it does offer a mechanism for ensuring that the practice's financial data is arranged in proper financial statement format and is accompanied by an outside accountant's report.

Tax Services

Accountants provide a variety of tax services, most of which can be classified as either compliance or planning. *Tax compliance* includes the preparation of various tax returns and information returns, and advising clients of due dates and tax payments in accordance with the various tax laws of federal, state, and local governments. Accountants often represent their clients, usually for an additional fee, in the event a return is audited.

When performing *tax planning,* the accountant assists clients in arranging their transactions, business structure, and affairs in such a manner as to legally minimize their tax liability. Examples of tax planning include advice selecting the appropriate form of entity; structuring the timing, depreciation, and financing arrangements for asset acquisitions; and year-end tax planning.

Often, an outside accountant will prepare both the entity returns and the owners' individual returns. This helps facilitate tax planning, as physician-owned practices often have multiple related-party transactions. As advisor for both the business and the individual, the accountant gains a better understanding of the clients' total financial state of affairs. Conversely, some groups follow a policy of not using the same accountant for group matters that any group member uses personally. This can help avoid real or perceived conflicts; larger groups will inevitably have physicians who do not use the same accountant as the group.

Other Services

Because of their knowledge of practice operations gained from performing the basic tax and accounting services, accountants are often well-positioned to provide other services to their clients. For example, accountants frequently provide ongoing consulting on an as-needed basis, such as for advice regarding projections, contract negotiations, budgets, profitability studies, and other financial matters. Outside accountants who develop a relationship with a particular practice are not just familiar with that particular practice; they have the benefit of knowledge gained from their experiences with other medical groups and businesses in general.

Some accountants have developed niches in certain industries and areas. For example, many provide retirement plan administration, personal financial planning, or business valuation services. Some firms have developed an expertise in health care consulting and may perform billing audits, facilitate strategic planning, and other such services.

Some CPAs obtain specialist designations from the AICPA by completing certain education and experience requirements and passing a comprehensive exam. Only CPAs are eligible for these credentialing programs. These include the Personal Financial Specialist, Certified Information Technology Professional, and Accreditation in Business Valuation.

A forensic accountant specializes in investigating fraud. The Association of Certified Fraud Examiners confers the Certified Fraud

Examiner credential on individuals who meet certain academic and experience requirements and pass a comprehensive exam.

Bankers

A practice must have a bank account in order to operate, and most practices need to borrow money at some point in time. Today's banks offer services beyond checking accounts and loans, including trust departments, investment advisory services, mutual funds, credit card processing, and treasury management services.

Selecting a Bank

One consideration in selecting a bank is the convenience of its locations. Time spent driving across town to make deposits or pick up lockboxes can be expensive.

Another consideration is the bank's ability to provide treasury management services. Many practices improve their cash flow by using a sweep account that allows cash balances to earn a higher rate of interest right up until a disbursement clears the bank. Lockbox services can provide practices with improved internal control over cash receipts. (See discussion on internal controls in Chapter 2.)

Of course, fees are a consideration. Checking account charges and credit card processing fees vary, and charges for trust department and lockbox services (and the related lockbox service options) vary considerably.

Lending Relationship Considerations

Because banks frequently require a depository account in connection with a loan, the ability of a bank to provide the best financing arrangement can be the overriding factor in selecting a bank. Some practices maintain an ongoing relationship with two or more banks and obtain loan proposals from both (or all) of these banks in an attempt to obtain the best of both worlds – competitive bidding *and* ongoing relationships. Be aware, however, that maintaining too many bank accounts can complicate financial management.

When lending to physician practices, bankers may assess the practice's creditworthiness on a "global" basis – that is, they consider the combined the assets, debts, net worth, earnings, and contingent liabilities of the entity and its owners. Thus, financial problems of individual owners can adversely affect the practice's ability to obtain financing.

The fact that banks often require physician-owners to personally guarantee practice loans sometimes upsets physicians, particularly when the bank requests personal financial information and personal tax returns. The administrator should be prepared to explain that this is normal, especially with an unsecured line of credit. A bank may require less paperwork from the practice if a significant number of the practice's physician-owners conduct their personal banking with that bank. In the case of a secured loan, the bank may agree to issue the loan without the personal guarantees. Depending on the nature of the practice, the owners' individual financial situations, the bank, and the loan, the banker may agree to each owner guaranteeing only his or her pro rata share, rather than requiring each owner to guarantee the entire loan balance. Current trends in personal guarantees for medical practice lending include:

- The division of personal guarantees into a multiple of pro rata practice ownership; for example, a 150-percent pro rata guaranty equates to a 15-percent loan guaranty for a 10-percent owner;

- A concentration of guarantees in select partners (typically the most creditworthy), with side agreements between the guarantor and nonguarantor owners; and

- Quasi-guaranty agreements in which the owners establish a base level of compensation and subordinate excess profit distributions to the payment of debt

Particularly when obtaining financing, the practice benefits from working with a banker who is experienced in dealing with medical practices. Bankers who are accustomed to receiving accrual basis financial statements may balk at the cash basis financial statements prepared by most physician-owned practices. The fact that these financial statements often have low (or even negative) retained earnings – due to paying out substantially all of the practice's profits as bonuses to minimize income taxes – may bother these bankers even more. Finally, lenders who are not familiar with the health care industry may not understand the contractual write-offs associated with accounts receivable.

The Banker–Administrator Relationship

Bankers usually like to do business with physicians and medical practices but may have difficulty communicating with the physicians, who may be busy seeing patients or may fail to provide sufficient details when discussing financial matters. For this reason, bankers often look to the administrator to facilitate their relationship with the practice. Bankers prefer receiving a comprehensive packet of practice financial information to assist them in analyzing a potential loan and presenting the loan application to decision makers in the bank. In addition to copies of the practice's (and probably the owners') financial statements and tax returns, bankers generally need information regarding accounts receivable and payer mix. When financing major asset acquisitions or expansions, bankers usually want projections for both operations and cash flow. The administrator should anticipate questions the banker may have and be prepared to spend time explaining the practice's financial matters.

Attorneys

A medical practice should also retain the services of a competent attorney. To obtain a license to practice law, an attorney must earn a juris doctor (J.D.) degree and pass the bar exam. Some attorneys obtain advanced law degrees, such as an LLM (master of laws) in taxation. As is the case with accountants, attorneys may practice as sole practitioners or as members of a firm. Because legal work is often specialized, the practice may need to use more than one attorney. For example, the attorney who gives great guidance on human resource management issues may have a partner who handles retirement plan issues. Some firms have an entire department of attorneys dedicated to health care law.

In the financial arena, the attorney generally assists the practice in making decisions regarding entity selection and drafts the articles of incorporation, bylaws, employment contracts, and buy-sell agreements. If the practice has an individually written retirement plan (as opposed to a prototype plan), its attorney will typically draft the plan documents, including the required plan amendments.

The practice's attorney often works closely with the practice's accountant on matters concerning finance and taxation. In some cases, practice leaders might discuss a financial matter with their attorney instead of their accountant because of attorney-client privilege.

Medical practices typically consult their attorney on an ongoing basis for various legal matters such as contracts, compliance matters, and other sensitive issues. In deciding whether or not to consult an attorney, the practice should weigh the risks of making the wrong decision against the cost of preemptive legal advice.

Insurance Agents

Although one usually associates insurance agents with the Risk Management domain, their services sometimes overlap with financial management. This is particularly true for life insurance agents because life insurance products frequently have investment characteristics or are part of a financial plan. These advisors might also sell other investment products, such as mutual funds. Additionally, many life insurance sales representatives perform investment advisory services and financial planning.

The chartered life underwriter (CLU) credential designates a life insurance professional with at least three years of experience who has passed eight college-level courses on life insurance and estate planning and meets certain ethics requirements. A CLU must meet continuing education and ethics requirements to retain the designation.

A. M. Best Company provides ratings and analyses on insurance companies and their products and sells this information in various print and online publications. Often an agent will provide information on the Best ratings in connection with a proposal. Another potential source is the local library, which might subscribe to this service. Some agents are tied to one particular insurance company, while others are independent agents who can shop among different insurance companies to find the best fit for their customer.

▇ Investment Advisors and Financial Planners

As discussed in preceding sections of this chapter, several types of financial advisors may also offer financial planning and investment advice. Others operate strictly as financial planners and/or investment advisors. Some work in large national brokerage firms, while others have their own smaller firms. These individuals may have different credentials. Exhibit 28 provides basic information regarding some of the more popular credentials. For a comprehensive list of credentials, visit the National Association of Securities Dealers (NASD) Website (www.nasd.com).

Due Diligence on Investment Advisors

The NASD Website (www.nasd.com) contains a section that allows the general public to look up information regarding individual brokers and firms. This Website also contains a good deal of other useful information for investors, including links to the Investment Adviser Public Disclosure Website, and a list of state security agencies (both discussed further on).

Any investment advisor (including accountants, attorneys, brokers, and others) who receives compensation for giving investment advice and manages at least $25 million in assets must register with the Securities and Exchange Commission (SEC) as a registered investment advisor (RIA). The SEC maintains a database of the RIAs who sell securities. This information is available on the Investment Adviser Public Disclosure Website (www.adviserinfo.sec.gov).

Because investment advisors must also register with their state securities agency, the practice may contact its state agency for verification and information on investment advisors.

EXHIBIT 28

Investment Advisor Credentials

Acronym/Credential	Requirements
CFP (Certified Financial Planner)	▪ Pass a 10-hour examination
	▪ Three years' experience (five if no bachelor's degree); bachelor's degree required beginning in 2007.
CFA (chartered financial analyst)	▪ Pass three examinations on investment analysis and portfolio management
	▪ Three years' experience
ChFC (chartered financial consultant)	▪ Pass eight college-level courses in areas such as investments, insurance, taxes, estate planning
	▪ Three years' experience
PFS (personal financial specialist)	▪ Must be a CPA and AICPA member
	▪ Meet various requirements in (1) experience, (2) examination, and (3) lifelong learning based on a multiple entry point system. The candidate must earn a total of 100 points with a minimum amount in each of the three areas.
RIA (registered investment advisor)	▪ Not a credential (a registration requirement for certain investment advisors).

Other Considerations

Practice decision makers should understand how different advisors are compensated. Some advisors charge a fee for their advice. Others do not charge for their advice but earn commissions from selling investments. Some large firms compensate individual brokers based on the commissions they generate, while others pay based on the amount of assets the broker manages.

◾ Retirement Plan Advisors

Medical practices also retain outside advisors to help with their retirement plans in various capacities. Depending on the nature of the plan, the nature of the group, and the extent to which the group handles responsibilities in-house, a group may have outside parties act as plan trustees, handle plan administration, and/or manage the plan's investments.

If any outside party is managing or advising the practice regarding the investments, the same considerations previously discussed for selecting investment advisors apply. Additionally, the advisor should have experience selecting investments that are appropriate for a retirement plan.

If the outside party is the plan's third-party administrator, ensure that this advisor is experienced in working with retirement plans, and specifically with the type of plan that the practice has. If the outside party will be a trustee, then these same caveats apply – except that even higher standards of knowledge and trustworthiness are required.

A practice may decide to adopt a prototype plan. Make sure the group leadership likes the investments offered and the plan provisions, and that it does due diligence as it would for an investment advisor and third-party administrator.

◾ Real Estate Professionals

Building and occupancy costs represent a large component of overhead for many practices. In addition, investments in practice real estate can provide handsome returns and other opportunities for physicians and sometimes administrators.

Whether a practice leases or purchases real estate, either decision entails a long-term commitment with a large build-out investment and at least some risk (ownership comes with more risks). Because medical groups often stay in their facilities for at least 5 years and sometimes 15 years or longer, real estate decisions are long term. Such decisions may occur only once or twice during a physician's career.

When medical groups negotiate office leases or building contracts, the groups are often negotiating with seasoned real estate professionals who have substantial resources. Most physicians and many practice managers have little real estate experience.

For all of these reasons, it is often prudent for a practice to hire a real estate professional. The real estate representative's fee may be based on a brokerage arrangement or a consulting basis.

In brokerage arrangements, the seller pays a commission to the real estate professional. In the past, these arrangements generally resulted in the broker owing an exclusive fiduciary responsibility to the seller or lessor who paid the commission. Recently, real estate brokers have been entering into buyer/broker arrangements where, even though the broker is compensated by the seller or lessor, the broker's fiduciary responsibility, and thus the broker's loyalty, is to the buyer or lessee.

The group might also retain estate advisors on a consulting basis. In this arrangement, the group contracts directly with the real estate professional to advise and assist in the transaction. The advisor's compensation is based on a fixed fee or hourly basis.

When more than one medical group is attempting to jointly develop a medical office building project, it is often wise to hire a seasoned real estate developer to lead the transaction and assist in bringing the parties together. In such cases, the real estate developer may be compensated through a development fee or may become a partner in the real estate development.

Consultants

Medical practices use a variety of consultants – and their backgrounds and credentials vary significantly. Some consultants practice with large international firms, while others work as individuals.

Although they frequently use consultants to perform a wide variety of projects, practices are most often seeking to improve a particular area of their business or clinical operations. Situations in which a practice should consider using an outside consultant include:

- The nature of the function requires an outsider; for example, an outside billing audit in accordance with the practice's compliance plan.

- Outside expertise is needed, either because internal personnel do not have the necessary skills, or because the consultant has a rare level of expertise; for example, hiring a firm with a reputation in medical practice valuation to assist the practice in this area.

- The engagement concerns a sensitive matter that is best handled by a competent outside party.

In selecting a consultant, ensure that the individual or firm has the background specific to performing the job. For example, if a billing audit involves primarily coding issues, a Certified Professional Coder would likely be a better choice than a CPA. Conversely, if the billing audit involves analyzing internal control and financial transactions, the CPA would probably be a better choice. Beware of hiring a health care consultant with strictly a hospital background to advise a physician practice.

Word of mouth is often a good way to locate a consultant with expertise in a particular area. Additionally, ask the consultant to provide a list of references and then check them.

Summary

Medical practices require a number of outside financial advisors. Knowing which advisors to use and when to use them is important. In evaluating potential advisors, check their credentials. Referrals from existing advisors and other practices are helpful, as is checking references provided by the potential advisors. Finally, don't overlook the ability of the advisors to communicate with the physicians, the administrator, the various stakeholders, and the practice's other advisors.

Chapter 6 **Optimizing Contract Negotiations and Existing Contracts**

MANY PRACTICE MANAGERS sometimes consider payer contract analysis and negotiation to be a difficult process with a low probability of success. At the same time, payer contracting is a most critical aspect of the practice revenue cycle. Even if a practice is unable to successfully negotiate rates they believe are fair market, numerous other provisions in the contract, if left unclear or ambiguous (i.e., obligations of the provider to adhere to medical management and care processes or bill timely and accurately), could further erode reimbursement and adversely impact much needed practice revenue. Many practices, especially smaller practices, choose to not read contracts because they are lengthy and contain little opportunity for negotiating. Administrators should read contracts completely, and then communicate to the various departments, such as nursing, registration, billing, and collections, so key members of the practice understand their respective obligations for meeting the terms of the contract. As much as 20 percent of revenue can be lost through noncompliant activities, from denials to bundling of codes.

◼ Contract Management

While some general themes can be applied to contracting, almost every situation is different to some degree. These differences most frequently relate to the marketplace and the relative strengths and weaknesses of the negotiating parties. Yet there are many details to manage during the contracting process. To create discipline and reinforce consistency, practices can follow a suggested framework, which will improve the negotiations and help to effectively manage multiple payer agreements. The five steps are:

1. Preparation – getting organized;
2. Negotiation;
3. Implementation;
4. Operations; and
5. Auditing.

When viewed as part of a cycle, each of these five steps builds and improves on the next step. So once a practice has audited reimbursement, the preparation for the next round of negotiations is made easier because issues are better understood. Data is integral for effective contract negotiations and, if applied correctly, the process takes discipline. In this section, we will discuss Steps 1 and 2.

Step 1: Preparation

Getting organized is essential and there are many ways to approach it. Creating a checklist of items to follow through on during the process helps to ensure that all tasks are completed and establishes discipline into what can be a time-consuming overwhelming process. Additionally, practice managers who come knowledgeable and prepared to the negotiating table establish credibility with the health plan.

The practice manager's initial step is to evaluate the relative strengths and weaknesses of the practice and the payers in the negotiation arena. Critical questions that the manager should ask include:

- What is the practice's relative level of dominance in its market?
- How much competition for the practice exists?

- Does the practice feature a physician specialty or subspecialty with little or no competition?

- Is the level of patient and/or incoming referral satisfaction so high that an insurance payer is compelled to include the practice in its provider panel?

- Does the practice have special programs, such as disease management, evening hours, weekend clinics, hospitalist coverage, and so forth, which many patients and payers find attractive and unique?

- How important are the practice and the payer to the employers and health insurance brokers in your community? What other practice strengths and weaknesses could impact negotiations?

- What types of products do the health plans sell?

A second step is to evaluate the payer organization using a parallel set of questions. After evaluating the medical group's and payer's positions in the marketplace, the manager is in a much better position to evaluate the contract terms and prepare for negotiations.

A third step is to develop a set of guiding principles that inform the contracting team and process. An assessment reflecting the level of risk the practice is willing to accept (both financial and nonfinancial) helps identify "must haves" vs. "wants." If a practice knows that costs are increasing by 5 percent, one guiding principle may be to require a 5 percent weighted increase on all negotiations, either through utilization changes or rate increases. Including key nurses, physicians, and business staff when creating guiding principles serves to communicate negotiating details, and in the event the practice chooses to walk from a contract, key practice staff is involved.

A fourth step is to obtain financial information on the practice. Before the negotiations begin with the insurance plan, the practice manager should have a thorough understanding of the current profitability and issues associated with each contract. In fact, most of the work should occur before negotiations actually begin with the insurance company. Completing a payer assessment of some type allows different departments to weigh in on the performance of the payer, in areas such as business services, patient registration, clinical care, and referral management. Additionally, a complete review that includes patient volume by product, utilization by type, and product profitability vs. overall profitability is critical to establishing a complete picture of the payer's performance. As a rule of thumb, you cannot negotiate effectively unless you understand your baseline and know what to ask for.

Of course, this information might not be available for a new contract; in this case, the practice may be wise to refuse an evergreen clause until the insurance company proves themselves. Practices typically have more leverage with new payers than they realize. Entrants into the marketplace have the added pressure of establishing new networks; they need providers more than they need insurance companies.

Step 2: Negotiating Contract Language

Negotiating rates is only one component of the overall request. Negotiating risky language out of the contract, as well as removing ambiguous and vague language, is critical to ensuring that the contract performs as is understood. One way is to redline the contract with preferred language. Additionally, clarifying ambiguous language beforehand may allow the practice to obtain desired changes without negotiating them.

Because many sections of a contract require scrutiny and negotiation, the practice may want to seek legal counsel.

Areas of risk in contracts are:

1. **Type of plan and the payers.** Identifying the products included in the contract helps to clarify and document the rates by product. If it is necessary, and to limit any reimbursement confusion later when claims are audited, attach an exhibit to the agreement that lists the product name and rates. Get a copy of each card and plan description. You will want to separate insurance codes and rates for each product to better monitor volume, denials, and so forth. Ensure that indemnity business is not tied to your health maintenance organization or preferred provider organization rates; it should be reimbursed at 100 percent of billed charges because it is not being directed to your group. It is also important to

have strong definitions of who is the payer, plan, participant, an dso on. Weak definitions can cause health plans to sell their network to other payers and apply any rates. Silent and vague contract language is too risky; it is better to capture intent and seek clarity and conciseness.

2. **Medical necessity.** Make sure the contract specifies who makes clinical decisions – is it the physician or the plan's director? If it is the plan director, ask for language that allows both your medical director and the plan director to meet and discuss when there is a disagreement. In no way should the plan be allowed to deny the claim for medical necessity if you received prior authorization. For Emergency Medical Treatment and Active Labor Act cases, the medical director decides medical necessity because the physician is accountable to treat and stabilize a patient under federal law.

3. **Indemnification.** The words "hold harmless" are a red flag for "signer beware!" Plans like to include this one way of making sure physicians hold the plan harmless for their actions. The contract language should be reciprocal, however, so both parties hold each other harmless and indemnify the acts of each other.

4. **Claims payment.** It is critical to understand your state and federal laws for claims payment, particularly when the contract defaults to language governed by state law. Because self-funded plans do not have to comply with state laws, you need to specify time frames.

5. **Provider manual.** The operational details of the contract are contained in the provider manual. Payers are increasingly scaling back on the contract and adding to the provider manual. Stipulate that the plan makes no material changes to the provider manual without your written agreement, particularly on material items such as rate changes or medical management obligations.

6. **Termination and renewal.** Contracts commonly contain clauses that automatically renew the agreement for another year. It is preferable to have one-year agreements with the

top five payers (those responsible for 70 percent of payments to the practice), so language and rates can be renegotiated. This approach requires the practice to set up a tickler system to manage the renewal dates. If this is impossible, consider language that allows for a 90-day-out no cause.

7. **Access to records.** Payers frequently need to review medical records. Although this need is appropriate, sometimes contained in this provision are access rights to financial information not found on the HCFA1500, such as costs, and so forth. Avoid language such as "all" patient financial records.

8. **Appeals and denials.** If this section is not in the contract, review the provider manual. This area is increasingly important to understand. Because of requirements of prompt pay statutes to settle all claims within 30 to 45 days, payers automatically deny claims to meet their obligation under the law, thus forcing practices to use the denial process. Negotiating reasonable time frames for appealing and settling claims is critical to the practice's cash flow. As a negotiating tactic, track the frivolous denial, quantify the dollars, divide the amount by the payer's relative value unit (RVU), and inform the payer of the additional amount it will cost them to contract with the practice because of the added costs of reprocessing unnecessary denials.

9. **Compensation.** Specifying the payment type in the agreement is critical to being able to later audit payment correctness, so spell out rates for cases, immunizations, and lab work, and, if possible, create a list of claims scenarios for proof-of-claims hierarchy payment and attach it to the agreement. If the practice is paid on a resource-based relative value scale (RBRVS), list the conversion factor year, RVU year, and whether or not it has been adjusted for the three Geographic Practice Cost Indices – work, practice expense, and malpractice. It is preferable to use current RVUs and negotiate off a conversion rate. Remove "lesser of" language from agreements, unless you understand where the fee schedule is set and how reimbursement will be affected. The argument to

the health plan is that if the contract is based on agreed-upon rates, the payer should not be able to change them later, because this would affect the modeling of profitability of the contract. At the same time, be careful of usual and customary language in commercial contracts. Embedded in the calculation of usual and customary rates are reimbursement rates for Workers' Compensation, Medicaid, and Medicare. If the agreement states it is the lesser of usual and customary or the contracted rate, exactly what is included in reimbursement may be unclear.

10. **Governing law.** Make sure the governing law is in the state in which the physicians practice. Some of the national networks indicate their home state. This is not feasible for arbitration and claims payment and medical management requirements.

Reviewing contract language is a time-consuming, tedious process, but it is one that will produce better outcomes for the practice. Remember, it's not just about negotiating the rate; language that is disastrous to the practice impacts the net margin every time.

Before arranging for a meeting with a payer, the practice manager should be sure that he or she understands all of these areas, as well as the payer and its performance. The practice administrator should then arrive at the negotiations with a prepared proposal that includes rates and contract language.

Types of Contracts

Type of reimbursement routinely characterizes contracts between practices and payers. Payment schedules in these contracts have evolved over the years from "pay your full fees" to "pay discounted practice fees" to payer fee schedules to capitation risk and relative value payment schedules. Contracts also contain a variety of hybrid methodologies. Generally, a specific region follows an identifiable reimbursement theme, but the standard may be evolving to a newer methodology.

Basic Medicare and Medicaid do not generally negotiate contracts. They post their reimbursement rates and terms, and if the practice is a participating provider, the published rates apply.

Fee-for-service (FFS) contracts are fairly standard. Reimbursement is based on the type and number of services provided, but payment can be based on fee schedules (yours or the payers) that list the specific payment per procedure or are driven by an RVU system. The most common RVU system today is the Centers for Medicare and Medicaid Services RBRVS, but contracts with a popular predecessor, such as Ingenix (formerly known as St. Anthony's and as McGraw-Hill) can occasionally be found.

Risk contracts are generally paid on a capitation rate quoted as "$pmpm" (payment per member per month) for a range of services that the practice is responsible for providing to the enrollees. The range of services encompasses basic primary care to global care, which includes all physician, facility, and even pharmaceutical expenses. Generally, only large multispecialty physician groups affiliated with a hospital facility in some type of integrated arrangement would consider a global contract. Managing capitation risk is addressed in more detail in the following section.

Case rate contracting is agreeing to a fixed amount for a service or range of services. A specialty provider may agree to a fixed rate for an episode of care related to a specific diagnosis and have an FFS contract for all other services. A common example of this kind of contract is for OB/GYN services. The practice agrees to a fixed case rate for all deliveries and related services to include the pre- and postnatal visits and delivery regardless of methodology. All other services are covered under an FFS contract.

■ Managing Risk Contracts

Effective management of risk contracts can be daunting, and even experienced practice managers frequently retain outside assistance when the complexity and/or size of the contract warrants it. The payer has a stable of very experienced actuaries who constantly review the relationship between populations of patients of various ages by gender and the anticipated costs of treating these patients. The payer is likely to have much better data from which to negotiate reimbursement terms.

In theory, the payer's objective is to transfer the cost, or risk, of treating the patients to the physicians for a reasonable level of capitation. The payer then knows with a fair degree of certainty what it will cost to treat the patients for the scope of services under the capitation agreement. It is the practice manager's objective to negotiate for adequate capitation to cover the projected cost of services and provide some cushion to compensate for the inherent risk in these contracts. For this reason, many managers retain an actuarial firm to evaluate the payer's offer.

Understanding the scope of services for which the practice is responsible is critical. The list of services is generally documented on a "responsibility matrix" that identifies, by Current Procedural Terminology code range and/or description, the parties to the contract and their responsibilities. For instance, a capitation contract may divide the service and/or cost responsibilities between the physician group, a hospital facility, and the insurance plan. The practice administrator's job is to eliminate any ambiguity from the practice's responsibilities and evaluate the financial responsibilities of the proposal.

Understanding the scope of services is only part of the process. The manager also needs to evaluate the list of services to determine how much the practice can really influence the provision of these services and therefore manage costs. For example, a pediatric group may have to decide whether to absorb the risk of rising immunization costs, especially new immunizations. In this case the manager can estimate the number of immunizations required for a specific patient population, but may not be able to forecast the cost of drugs, especially new ones.

Stop-loss insurance is one way for the practice to protect itself from unanticipated utilization and expense. One type of stop-loss insurance would reimburse the practice for all or a portion of expenses related to a specific patient exceeding a threshold amount of $25,000. Another type could limit the practice's total costs to a fixed amount "$pmpy" (payment per member per year). Knowing what type and how much, if any, insurance to purchase is another actuarial exercise.

Contracting and Health Care Law

The legal aspects of contracting add an additional complexity to the process. In addition to issues related to the actual contract document, government regulations impact certain contracting behaviors.

Addressing the government regulations first, many of these rules fall under the antitrust laws that prohibit a number of anti-competitive acts. Practice mergers and joint ventures, price fixing, market allocations, and various collaborative agreements between competing practices to boycott payers or set reimbursement and contract terms might be construed to be violations of the various regulations.

The actual contract between the practice and payer requires careful review. The practice manager should not hesitate to obtain legal assistance, preferably from an experienced health care attorney, to evaluate the contract terms. One can assume that a contract presented by the payer and drawn up by the payer's legal firm might be at least a little one-sided in favor of the payer.

Some specific areas to approach with particular caution relate to dispute resolution, termination mechanisms and responsibilities, indemnification of the other party (usually the payer), payment terms, unilateral change provisions, and references to other documents that are considered to part of the contract, such as a provider manual. This list can go on considerably, and the practice manager needs to be aware of the potential traps within contracts.

Negotiating contract terms goes beyond just setting reimbursement rates. Do not be afraid to challenge contract clauses that are unfair to the practice. In many cases the payer will have alternative and more equitable language if requested.

Health Care Standards

Payer contracts have become more complex over the years. Some payers (not all) have evolved from the basic pay for services to utilization and quality management. Although the line between utilization management and quality improvement can be blurry, there is no doubt that many payers and accrediting organizations are becoming increasingly interested in how health care is delivered.

Utilization management attempts to limit the frequency of inappropriate or unnecessary health care. Payers profile physicians and reward or penalize providers for performance. A risk contracting method is to track the number of hospital days per 1,000 members per year. Although the payer or facility is at financial risk, it is easily recognized that physicians drive the number of admissions and the length of a hospital stay. The providers might be rewarded or penalized for their length of hospital stay per thousand performance. Some argue that tracking this data is a perverse incentive to physicians to prematurely discharge or not admit sicker patients in order to meet benchmarks.

Today, many programs are designed to improve the quality of care. Some of these focus on disease management and quality improvement initiatives. Improved patient satisfaction is also a standard against which physicians can be measured. Organizations such as the National Committee for Quality Assurance, the Joint Commission on Accreditation of Healthcare Organizations, and many others are promoting their benchmarks for the delivery of quality health care. Pay-for-performance programs reward physician groups for meeting certain quality goals.

Contract Negotiations: Techniques and Tactics

Effectively negotiating contracts is both an art and a science. The most skillful negotiators are not only extremely prepared and savvy, they balance their knowledge of the practice's needs with respect for the payer's position. Negotiating contracts is about building and maintaining relationships. Because at some point after the negotiations have ended, problems need resolving and a positive relationship between the practice and the payer facilitates this process.

The following recommendations are not intended to be all inclusive but are suggestions to start and build a comfort level with what is considered a difficult process by many managers.

- **Be prepared with data.** The side with the most data to support its position doesn't always win, but preparation can be an advantage. As mentioned earlier, bring a checklist of items to help guide the discussions. Some requests may be standard contract items and others may be specific to the practice's past experience – both positive and negative – of the health plan.

- **Meet face to face if you can.** When people meet face to face, something happens that cannot occur in a phone conversation. The practice has a better chance of getting what it wants, establishing a relationship, and putting together a contract in a face-to-face meeting with the payer. Time should be used wisely, however, so come to negotiations prepared to discuss the details of the deal. Also, take good notes and document the intent of the parties, so you have material to review when it comes to committing the concepts to writing.

- **Be aware of your negotiating style and how it is seen by the other party.** Are you too loud and demanding or excessively meek and mild? What can you expect from the other negotiating party? Cooperation or combat?

- **Stay focused on your objectives and goals.** Goal setting should occur jointly between the provider and payer. Understanding the other party's interests and issues helps create a better contract. For example, the payer may not be able to give you a rate increase, but it may be able to give you something else that is important, such as added providers or services that were not previously covered. Although the rate per se didn't increase, the overall value and profitability may have increased. Sometimes changing contract language and provider obligations is more important than anything else.

- **Define the deal breakers.** What is absolutely necessary for the contract to work? What can be conceded? It's important to recognize that negotiations begin once offers have been made. It is not mandatory to negotiate if an offer is favorable. At times it is preferable to let the payer make the first offer; it allows insights into where they believe the market competitive rates lie.

- **Be professional.** Using courtesy, negotiate only on a win/win basis. Show a genuine interest in the payer's position. Do not allow yourself to become emotional in the negotiating process; one way to do this is to negotiate as a team.

- **Be inventive.** It is one of the most useful assets a negotiator can learn, but it requires looking at the entire package being offered.

- **Persevere.** If the practice doesn't get what it wants, keep it on the list and ask for it again and again. People may change, but the practices issues may not.

Summary

Proper preparation can make the process of negotiating third-party contracts less stressful. Knowledge of the market and the relative strengths and weaknesses of the negotiating parties is the foundation for successful contracting. Negotiating skills can be learned through practice, and, with persistence and the ability to listen, a negotiator can create options and improve the odds for success. The next building block is to have a working understanding of the pros and cons related to the various types of contracts and payment mechanisms. Special attention is required for risk contracting and the complexities involved with capitation. Understanding and negotiating the contract are the final steps to making a contract official. Remember, having a contract in place is one thing; the payer living up to its side of the agreement is another. Constant evaluation of the contractual performance is the foundation for renegotiation when the time comes.

Exercises

THESE QUESTIONS have been retired from the ACMPE Essay Exam question bank. Because there are so many ways to handle various situations, there are no "right" answers and, thus, no answer key. Use these questions to help your practice respond to different scenarios.

1. You are the administrator for a medical practice in which one of the physicians has historically produced greater than 50 percent of the total group productivity. He recently sold his shares back to the practice in preparation for a two-year phaseout to retirement. Three months into the transition, the physician became totally and permanently disabled.

   Describe how you would handle this situation.

2. You are the administrator of a 10-physician primary care group. One of your top-producing family practitioners comes to you and requests an additional nurse or medical assistant. The physician claims that he will be able to increase his productivity substantially if given the additional help.

    Discuss how you would evaluate the request and describe your recommended course of action.

3. You are the new administrator of a busy six-physician general surgery practice. The physicians also treat trauma patients at a large inner city hospital. The practice has three months in receivables and the percentage of receivables greater than 120 days is 30 percent.

   Describe how you would handle this situation.

4. You are the administrator of a medical group. The group has been experiencing an increase in its health insurance premiums. One of your group's physicians, newly elected to the board, asked if it were feasible to self-insure all or a portion of this benefit for the group. In response, you have been asked by the board to analyze the risks and benefits of self-insuring this benefit.

What course of action would you take in this situation?

5. You are the new chief operating officer of a large multispecialty group with a number of locations. As chief operating
   officer, you report to the executive board and are administratively responsible for all business operations. In your first
   week on the job, the business manager asks to schedule an
   appointment with you. The business manager reports that
   one of the locations is having trouble getting its daily post-
   ings completed. Charges are not being entered in a timely
   manner, bank deposits are made sporadically, demographic
   information is not regularly updated, and coding errors are
   frequent. In the course of the conversation, you discover
   that all offices have similar problems and are making little
   effort to correct the processes, even though they have been
   notified repeatedly by the business manager about the
   issues.

   What course of action would you take in this situation?

6. You are the administrator of a large multispecialty medi-
    cal group. You have 15 employees in the billing office. You
    have just received a call from the bank where your deposits
    are made that the employee responsible for making depos-
    its has just made a deposit into her own account consisting
    of several insurance checks made out to the group.

    How would you handle this situation?

Appendices

APPENDIX 3.1

DEEP SOUTH OBSTETRICS AND GYNECOLOGY, P.C.
Benchmark Against MGMA Cost Survey
Overall per FTE Physician
2003

		20X3			
	Practice $	Practice $ Per FTE Physician	MGMA Cost Benchmark	Practice Over (Under) MGMA Benchmark $	%
Revenues:					
Net fee-for-service revenue	$4,980,000	$711,429	$663,067	$48,362	7.3%
Capitation revenue					
Other	270,000	38,571	5,505	33,066	600.7%
Net revenue	5,250,000	750,000	668,572	81,428	12.2%
Operating Expenses					
Salaries and benefits					
Staff salaries	1,246,000	178,000	140,858	37,142	26.4%
Employee benefits and taxes	295,000	42,143	37,492	4,651	12.4%
Total salaries and benefits (sum of above)	1,541,000	220,143	178,350	41,793	23.4%
Total salaries and benefits (from survey)			172,199	47,944	27.8%
Services and General Expenses					
Malpractice insurance	310,000	44,286	36,834	7,452	20.2%
Medical and surgical supplies	173,000	24,714	17,284	7,430	43.0%
Depreciation	75,000	10,714	4,695	6,019	128.2%
Amortization	5,000	714	714		
Rent	330,000	47,143	42,052	5,091	12.1%
Information technology	90,000	12,857	10,074	2,783	27.6%
Other general and administrative expenses	157,000	22,429	49,693	(27,264)	−54.9%
Total services and general expenses (sum of above)	1,140,000	162,857	160,632	2,225	1.4%
Total services and general expenses (from survey)			177,896	(15,039)	−8.5%

APPENDIX 3.1 *(continued)*

DEEP SOUTH OBSTETRICS AND GYNECOLOGY, P.C.
Benchmark Against MGMA Cost Survey
Overall per FTE Physician
2003

	Practice $	20X3 Practice $ Per FTE Physician	20X3 MGMA Cost Benchmark	20X3 Practice Over (Under) MGMA Benchmark $	20X3 Practice Over (Under) MGMA Benchmark %
Provider-related expenses					
Physician salaries	1,865,000	266,429	220,210	46,219	21.0%
Physician benefits and taxes	450,000	64,286	41,526	22,760	54.8%
Total physician costs	2,315,000	330,714	261,736	68,978	26.4%
Nurse practitioner salaries	196,000	28,000	28,713	(713)	−2.5%
Nurse practitioner benefits and taxes	49,000	7,000	6,492	508	7.8%
Total nurse practitioner costs	245,000	35,000	35,205	(205)	−0.6%
Total provider costs (sum of above)	2,560,000	365,714	296,941	68,773	23.2%
Total provider costs (from survey)			318,938	46,776	14.7%
Total Operating Expenses	5,241,000	748,714	635,923	112,791	17.7%
Income from Operations	9,000	1,286			
Nonmedical costs					
Interest and taxes	(10,000)	(1,429)	(6,710)	5,281	−78.7%
Income (Loss)	$(1,000)	$(143)	$2,865	$(3,008)	−105.0%
FTE Physicians	7				
FTE NPP	3				

MGMA Cost Benchmark from MGMA *Cost Survey, 2004 Report Based on 2003 Data,* Tables 13.4b–13.4e.

APPENDIX 3.2

DEEP SOUTH OBSTETRICS AND GYNECOLOGY, P.C.
Benchmark Against MGMA Cost Survey
Overall Percent of Total Medical Revenue
2003

	20X3				
	% of Total Medical Revenue				
	Practice		MGMA	Practice Over (Under) MGMA	
	$	%	Benchmark	% Points	%
Revenues:					
Net fee-for-service revenue	$4,980,000	94.9%	99.9%	−5.0%	−5%
Capitation revenue					
Other	270,000	5.1%	0.1%	5.0%	5043%
Net revenue	5,250,000	100.0%	100.0%	0.0%	0%
Operating Expenses					
Salaries and benefits					
Staff salaries	1,246,000	23.7%	21.3%	2.4%	11%
Employee benefits and taxes	295,000	5.6%	5.5%	0.1%	2%
Total salaries and benefits					
(sum of above)	1,541,000	29.4%	26.8%	2.6%	10%
Total salaries and benefits					
(from survey)			26.9%	2.4%	9%
Services and General Expenses					
Malpractice insurance	310,000	5.9%	5.5%	0.4%	7%
Medical and surgical supplies	173,000	3.3%	2.8%	0.5%	16%
Depreciation	75,000	1.4%	0.6%	0.8%	142%
Amortization	5,000	0.1%	0.1%		
Rent	330,000	6.3%	7.1%	-0.8%	−11%
Information technology	90,000	1.7%	1.6%	0.1%	7%
Other general and					
administrative expenses	157,000	3.0%	7.4%	-4.4%	−60%
Total services and general					
expenses (sum of above)	1,140,000	21.7%	25.1%	−3.3%	−13%
Total services and general					
expenses (from survey)			25.3%	-3.6%	−14%

APPENDIX 3.2 *(continued)*

DEEP SOUTH OBSTETRICS AND GYNECOLOGY, P.C.
Benchmark Against MGMA Cost Survey
Overall Percent of Total Medical Revenue
2003

	20X3				
	% of Total Medical Revenue				
	Practice		MGMA	Practice Over (Under) MGMA	
	$	%	Benchmark	% Points	%
Provider-related expenses					
Physician salaries	1,865,000	35.5%	35.9%	−0.3%	−1%
Physician benefits and taxes	450,000	8.6%	6.4%	2.2%	35%
Total physician costs	2,315,000	44.1%	41.9%	2.2%	5%
Nurse practitioner salaries	196,000	3.7%	3.7%	0.1%	1%
Nurse practitioner benefits					
and taxes	49,000	0.9%	0.8%	0.1%	17%
Total nurse practitioner costs	245,000	4.7%	4.8%	−0.1%	−3%
Total provider costs					
(sum of above)	2,560,000	48.8%	48.8%	0.0%	0%
Total provider costs					
(from survey)			45.7%	3.0%	7%
Total Operating Expenses	5,241,000	99.8%	99.8%	0.0%	0%
Income from Operations	9,000	0.2%			
Nonmedical costs					
Interest and taxes	(10,000)	−0.2%	−1.0%	1.0%	−100%
Income (Loss)	(1,000)	0.0%	0.1%	−0.1%	−133%

MGMA Cost Benchmark from MGMA Cost Survey, *2004 Report Based on 2003 Data*, Tables 13.5a–13.5d.

APPENDIX 3.3

DEEP SOUTH OBSTETRICS AND GYNECOLOGY, P.C.
Benchmark Against MGMA Cost Survey
Staffing per FTE Physician
2003

	FTE Practice	FTE per FTE Physician	MGMA Cost Benchmark	Practice Over (Under) MGMA Benchmark	
				FTE	%
General administrative					
Administrator	1.00	0.14			
Secretary	1.00	0.14			
Total general administrative	2.00	0.29	0.28	0.01	2%
Patient accounting					
Patient accounting manager	1.00	0.14			
Patient accounting staff	4.00	0.57			
Total patient accounting	5.00	0.71	0.67	0.04	7%
General accounting	0.00	0.00	0.08	−0.08	
Medical receptionists	7.00	1.00	1.05	−0.05	−5%
Medical secretaries, transcribers	2.00	0.29	0.23	0.06	24%
Medical records	3.00	0.43	0.38	0.05	13%
Other administrative support	0.00	0.00	0.17	−0.17	
Total administrative support staff (sum of above)	19.00	2.71	2.86	−0.15	−5%
Total administrative support staff (from survey)			2.57	0.14	6%
Clinical support staff					
Registered nurses	4.00	0.57	0.43	0.14	33%
Licensed practical nurses	2.00	0.29	0.42	−0.13	−32%
Medical assistants, nurses aides	6.00	0.86	0.92	−0.06	−7%
Total clinical support (sum of above)	12.00	1.71	1.77	−0.06	−3%
Total clinical support (from survey)			1.70	0.01	1%
Ancillary support staff					
Clinical laboratory	1.50	0.21	0.20	0.01	7%
Radiology and imaging	3.50	0.50	0.22	0.28	127%
Total ancillary support staff (sum of above)	5.00	0.71	0.42	0.29	70%
Total ancillary support staff(from survey)					
Grand total staff (sum of above)	36.00	5.14	5.05	0.09	2%
Grand total staff (from survey)			4.62	0.52	11%
FTE Physicians	7				
FTE NPP	3				

MGMA Cost Benchmark from MGMA *Cost Survey, 2004 Report Based on 2003 Data*, Table 13.4a.

APPENDIX 3.4

DEEP SOUTH OBSTETRICS AND GYNECOLOGY, P.C.
Benchmark Against MGMA with Compensation
2003

Physician/Extender	Days Off	Practice Type	Professional Charges	Collections
Smith	45	GYN	650,000	300,000
% of Benchmark	129%		93%	92%
Jones	40	GYN	800,000	425,000
% of Benchmark	114%		115%	130%
MGMA Median	35		696,255	327,192
Harris	32	OB/GYN	1,200,000	600,000
% of Benchmark	91%		137%	115%
Thruman	30	OB/GYN	1,300,000	675,000
% of Benchmark	86%		148%	129%
Dunn	20	OB/GYN	1,500,000	750,000
% of Benchmark	57%		171%	144%
Thompson	25	OB/GYN	1,200,000	600,000
% of Benchmark	71%		137%	115%
Cohen	30	OB/GYN	1,200,000	650,000
% of Benchmark	86%		137%	125%
MGMA Median	35		877,845	521,418
Nurse Practitioner				
Bence	20	Office	225,000	175,000
% of Benchmark			99%	115%
Davis	25	Office	200,000	155,000
% of Benchmark			88%	102%
MGMA Median			227,188	152,215
Starr	25	Hospital		
Total Nurse Practitioner			227,188	152,215

MGMA Benchmark from MGMA *Physician Compensation and Production Survey, 2004 Report Based on 2003 Data,*
Tables 23, 43, 50, 52, 54 and 2.

	Encounters			Hospital			Total
Office	Hospital	Total	Cases	Ultrasounds	RVUs	Comp.
2,000	75	2,075	125	275	7,500	225,000
87%	99%	87%	93%	0%	86%	140%
2,400	115	2,515	175	325	9,000	225,000
104%	151%	106%	130%	0%	103%	140%
2,298	76	2,374	135	–	8,724	160,510
3,100	140	3,240	310	350	12,000	270,000
103%	100%	103%	94%	0%	103%	115%
3,500	155	3,655	325	375	12,500	280,000
116%	111%	116%	99%	0%	107%	119%
3,750	210	3,960	375	425	13,750	325,000
124%	150%	125%	114%	0%	118%	138%
3,100	135	3,235	300	325	12,000	265,000
103%	96%	103%	91%	0%	103%	113%
3,050	150	3,200	315	350	12,300	275,000
101%	107%	101%	96%	0%	105%	117%
3,016	140	3,156	329	-	11,661	235,000
2,200					6,000	65,000
137%					125%	104%
2,400					5,500	65,000
149%					114%	104%
1,607					4,818	62,789
						66,000
1,607	–	–	–	–	4,818	196,000

Notes

1. Ernest Pavlock, *Financial Management for Medical Groups* (Denver, CO: Medical Group Management Association, 1994), 8.

2. Reprinted from *MGMA Connexion*, Vol. 5, Issue 4, April 2005, with permission of Medical Group Management Association. All rights reserved.

3. The sample budget worksheets in this chapter were adapted from *Cost Management and Cost Accounting in the Medical Practice*, A 2006 MGMA Preconference Program, presented by Frederic R Simmons, CPA, and Lee Ann Webster, MA, CPA, FACMPE; Las Vegas, NV; Oct. 22, 2006.

4. Charles T. Horngren, Srikant M. Datar, and George Foster, *Cost Accounting: A Managerial Emphasis* (Upper Saddle River, NJ: Prentice Hall, 2002), 193.

5. Greg Brue and Rod Howes. *The McGraw-Hill 36-Hour Course: Six Sigma* (New York: McGraw-Hill, 2006), 59.

6. Horngren, Datar, and Foster, 178.

7. Neill F. Piland, Dr. P.H., and Kathryn P. Glass, *Chart of Accounts for Health Care Organizations* (Englewood, CO: Center for Research in Ambulatory Health Care Administration, 1999).

8. Ibid.

9. Internal Revenue Service, *Publication 946: How to Depreciate Property*. 2005.

10. Internal Revenue Service, Form 4562 Instructions: 2006.

11. Horngren, Datar, and Foster, 3.

12. Ibid.

13. This example was adapted from *Cost Management and Cost Accounting in the Medical Practice*, A 2006 MGMA Preconference Program, presented by Lee Ann H. Webster and Frederic R. Simmons Jr., Las Vegas, NV; Oct. 22, 2006.

14. Horngren, Datar, and Foster, 836.

15. Ibid., 837.

16. Ibid., 31.

17. Committee of Sponsoring Organizations of the Treadway Commission. Internal Control – Integrated Framework (July 1994), 13.

18. Ibid., 3.

19. Ibid., 33.

20. Ibid., 43–46.

21. Ibid., 49.

22. William E. Thompson, *Internal Controls: Design and Documentation* (Englewood, CO: Micromash, 2006).

23. Ibid., 76–77.

24. Lawrence Wolper, *Physician Practice Management: Essential Operational and Financial Knowledge* (Englewood, CO: Medical Group Management Association, 2005), 374.

25. Ibid., 453–454.

26. Ibid., 280.

27. Ibid., 314.

28. Ibid., 332.

29. Deborah Walker, Sara M. Larch, and Elizabeth W. Woodcock, *The Physician Billing Process: Avoiding Potholes in the Road to Getting Paid* (Englewood, CO: Medical Group Management Association, 2004).

30. Ibid., 47.

31. Ibid., 57.

32. Ibid., 218.

33. Brue and Howes, 43.

34. These sample financial statements were adapted from the MGMA 2005 Annual Conference Breakout Session "Financial Statements 101," presented by Lee Ann H. Webster.

35. Rob Gold, "Coding Structure of the Chart of Accounts," in *Chart of Accounts for Health Care Organizations,* ed. Neill F. Piland, Dr. P.H., and Kathryn P. Glass (Englewood, CO: Center for Research in Ambulatory Health Care Administration, 1999), 20–27.

36. Thomas P. Edmonds, Frances M McNair, Edward E. Milam, and Philip R. Olds, *Fundamental Financial Accounting Concepts* (New York: McGraw-Hill, 2003), 582–583.

37. Medical Group Management Association, *MGMA Cost Survey 2006 Report Based on 2005 Data* (Englewood, CO: Medical Group Management Association, 2006).

38. American Institute of Certified Public Accountants, *AICPA Audit and Accounting Guide: Health Care Organization* (New York: American Institute of Certified Public Accountants, 2006).

39. M. Ramos, *Preparing and Reporting on Cash and Tax Basis Financial Statements* (New York: American Institute of Certified Public Accountants, 1998), 3.

40. Ibid., 3–11.

41. American Institute of Certified Public Accountants, *Audit Risk Alerts: Health Care Industry Developments — 2003/04* (New York: American Institute of Certified Public Accountants, 2003), 76.

42. "HealthSouth: The Accountancy Fraud," www.uow.edu.au/arts/ bmartin.dissent/documents/health/healthsouth (accessed Jan. 24, 2007).

43. Medical Group Management Association, *Cost Survey for Single-Specialty Practices, 2008 Report Based on 2007 Data* (Englewood, CO: Medical Group Management Association, 2006), 74.

44. Ibid., 90.

45. Ibid., 162, 204, 218.

46. Ibid., 46, 132, 148, 162.

47. Medical Group Management Association, *Cost Survey for Multispecialty Practices, 2008 Report Based on 2007 Data* (Englewood, CO: Medical Group Management Association, 2008), 26.

48. Medical Group Management Association, *2008 Cost Survey for Single-Specialty Practices*, 136.

49. Ibid., 136, 166.

50. Ibid., 77, 178, 221.

51. *Webster's New Collegiate Dictionary* (Copyright 1981 by G. & C. Merriam Co.).

52. David T. Kerns, "Quality Improvement Begins at the Top," *World* 20, Vol. 2 (5) (May 1986).

53. These examples were adapted from *Cost Management and Cost Accounting in the Medical Practice,* A 2006 MGMA Preconference Program, presented by Frederic R. Simmons and Lee Ann H. Webster; Las Vegas, NV; Oct. 22, 2006.

54. David Weinberger, "The Hyperlinked Organization" in *The Cluetrain Manifesto* by Rick Levine, Christopher Locke, Doc Searls, and David Weinberger (New York: Perseus Publishing, 2000, 2001), 129.

55. Michael Ramos, *Fraud Detection in a GAAS Audit: SAS No. 99 Implementation Guide* (New York: American Institute of Certified Accountants, 2000), 5–9.

56. *Codification of Statements on Standards for Accounting and Review Services* (New York: American Institute of Certified Public Accountants).

57. Ibid.

58. Ray Whittington, *Analytical Procedures for Small Business Engagements*, An AICPA Self-Study Course (Lewisville, TX: American Institute of Certified Public Accountants, 2005).

Glossary

accounts payable: Amounts on open account owed by the organization to outside persons or entities for goods and services received by the organization. These accounts are usually control accounts for individual accounts payable balances that may be contained in a subsidiary ledger.

accounts receivable (A/R): The open account amounts (debts) owed to the organization by other entities (including customers, patients, and third-party payers) as a result of the services provided to its customers and patients. Amounts assigned to "accounts receivable" are due to "gross fee-for-service charges." Assignment of a charge into A/R is initiated at the time an invoice is submitted for payment. For example, if an obstetrics practice establishes an open account for accumulation of charges when a patient is accepted into a prenatal program, and the charges will not be posted until after delivery, then A/R will not reflect these charges until an invoice is created. Deletion of charges from A/R is done when the account is paid, turned over to a collection agency, or written off as bad debt. "Accounts payable (refunds) to patients and payers" are subtracted from A/R before reporting A/R.

A/R write-offs: Differences between adjusted gross charges and the amount actually collected as settlements for particular accounts. These write-offs may be the result of negotiating a payment less than adjusted gross charges with an individual patient or third-party agency (contractual adjustment).

accrual: An accounting method where revenues are recorded as earned when services are performed rather than when cash is received. Cost is recorded in the period during which it is incurred, that is, when the asset or service is used, regardless of when cash is paid. Costs for goods and services that will be used to produce revenues in the future are reported as assets and recorded as costs in future periods. The accrual method balance sheet includes not only the assets and liabilities from the cash basis balance sheet, but also the receivables from patients, prepayments, and deferrals of costs, accruals of costs and revenues, and payables owed to suppliers.

accrued liabilities: Current liabilities accrued at the end of an accounting period to reflect the proper amount of expenses for the organization under the accrual basis of accounting. Generally, no invoices or other billings are received within the accounting period, and the liability for these items is estimated or obtained from other sources.

accrued payroll liabilities: Actual or estimated liabilities for payroll obligations. These accounts are credited (increased) when the payroll expense is incurred and are debited (decreased) when payment is made to the appropriate employee, agency, or authority.

adjustment: Adjustments represent the value of services performed for which payment is not expected to be received.

advances from settlements due to third-party agencies: Amounts owed to third-party agencies for current financing and other advances that are due and payable within one year. An example of a settlement due to a third-party agency would include amounts owed Medicare or Medicaid resulting from overpayments due to inaccurate claims.

allowance for change in net unrealized gains/losses on investments: For-profit medical organizations should record changes in fair market value of investments that are classified as "available for sale" in this account.

allowance for charity care: An account that tracks the patient services in which payment was neither sought nor collected by request of an authority (such as a physician or executive manager) within the organization or hospital.

allowance for estimated uncollectible receivables: Estimated amount of uncollectible receivables. A historical analysis of bad debt write-offs as well as contractual adjustments is usually required to determine periodic credits to this account.

amortization: As a general rule, amortization is used to record the consumption or utilization over time of intangible property. Accumulated amortization is a contra-account to the related intangible asset. Amortization is recorded periodically, that is monthly, as an expense of the profit/loss or income statement. The offsetting entry is to increase (credit) accumulated amortization.

assets: Resources owned by the business. Assets may be tangible (physical in character) such as land, buildings, and equipment, or a direct right to tangible property such as amounts due from patients and third-party agencies, or they can be intangible such as goodwill, patents, licenses, and leaseholds.

bad debt expense: This account is used for uncollectible accounts receivable and notes receivable. A historical analysis of bad debt write-offs is usually required to determine periodic credits to this account. Other methods may be used, but a consistent and justifiable method of estimating the periodic charge to provision for bad debts (and the corresponding credit to either the "allowance for estimated uncollectible receivables" account or the "allowance for bad debts patients" account) should be applied systematically.

bad debt recovery: Recovered revenues from collections that were originally written off as bad debt.

balance sheet: It is a snapshot of the financial situation on a given date. Also known as the statement of financial position because it lists the organization's assets, liabilities, and equity (capital) at a particular point in time.

bank overdrafts payable: Overdrafts on banks having no other free balances in amounts sufficient to offset.

bonus: Managed care contracts may have provisions for a bonus that would be paid after the accounts are reconciled at year end. Bonuses are commonly linked to the achievement of predetermined goals typically based on either total plan performance or on the reduction of medical expenses.

business corporation: A legal entity whose shareholders do not need to be licensed to practice the profession practiced by the corporation.

capital contributed in excess of par: Capital contributed by owners in excess of the par or stated value of the capital stock.

capitalization: Expensing of the costs of furniture, fixtures, and equipment over time. A common criterion for capitalization is a unit cost of $500 or more. Other criteria for capitalization include:

- A unit cost sufficiently large to justify the cost of control incident to an equipment or property ledger;

- Depreciable life of two years or more but less than the life of buildings to which the equipment or fixtures may be affixed;

- Use in organizational operations; and

- Sufficient individuality and size to make control feasible by means of identification tags or numbers.

capitated premium revenues – commercial: Net revenue actually collected from capitation payments, risk-sharing revenues, and other revenues paid to the organization by a health maintenance organization for assigned enrollees under a patient care contract.

capitation: A set amount of money received or paid out according to a managed care contract. Also known as a "cap rate," capitation is based on the number of enrollees in a health plan (membership) rather than on actual services delivered. It is usually expressed in units of per-member per-month. A health plan may adjust the capitation rate based on such factors as age and sex of the enrollee. A capitation contract is one in which the practice agrees to provide medical services to a defined population for a fixed price per beneficiary per month, regardless of the actual services provided. Capitated contracts, which always contain an element of risk, include commercial health maintenance organization, Medicare, and Medicaid capitation contracts.

cash – restricted: Cash that is limited for other than general operating purposes. Even though the cash may be restricted for use with noncurrent budget items, it may still be expended within one year.

cash – unrestricted: This account is for cash that is typically used for general operating purposes. Unrestricted cash on hand covers both a change fund and/or a petty cash fund. Unrestricted cash on deposit in banks is immediately available for current operations.

cash basis accounting: An accounting method where revenues are recorded when cash is received and costs are recorded when cash is paid out. Receivables, payables, accruals, and deferrals arising from operations are ignored. On a pure cash basis, long-lived (fixed) assets are expensed when acquired, leaving cash and investments as the only assets, and borrowings and payroll withholdings as the only liabilities.

cash surrender value of life insurance policies: Amounts that recognize the accumulated value inside a life insurance policy that could be used for loan purposes and/or that would be available upon the termination of a policy.

charity care: Patient care where no payment is expected or collected.

claims payable incurred but not reported: Liability account used to record an estimation of the amounts owed to providers outside the organization for medical services to prepaid patients of the organization for which invoices have not been received. These are normally estimated using historical lag factors. When invoiced, the claims should be transferred to contract claims payable.

collection agency write-offs: Any accounts turned over to a collection agency. The corresponding accounts receivable should be credited.

common stock: A type of stock whereby equity claims are held by the "residual owners" of the organization, who are the last to receive any distribution of earning or assets. It represents the stated or par value of stock issued to owners.

community health center: An ambulatory clinic serving an area with limited health services or with special health needs. The funding authority for these centers occurs under the Public Health Service Act. Community health centers coordinate federal, state, and local resources in a single organization capable of delivering both health care and related social services to a defined population. Although such centers may not directly provide all types of health care, they arrange for all medical services needed by their patients.

contract claims payable: This account is related to claims payable incurred but not reported. Once determined or invoiced, the contract claims from that account should be transferred to this account. Contract claims payable records amounts owed by the organization to providers outside the organization for medical services to patients assigned to the organization.

contributions: Amounts paid out by the organization to recognized nonprofit entities or to charitable causes.

coordination of benefits: Policy guidance within the National Association of Insurance Commissioners to prevent double payment for services when an enrollee has coverage from two or more sources. It is used to ensure that the insured's benefits from all sources do not exceed 100 percent of that allowable.

copayments (co-pays): Revenues generated from payment-sharing arrangements between the insurance carriers or federal entity and the patient, which often includes the concept of a specific amount of money per visit.

corporation: A for-profit organization recognized by law as a business entity separate and distinct from its shareholders. A medical practice organized as a corporation can either be a C corporation or an S corporation as designated by the Internal Revenue Code. The primary difference between these two types of entities is the way they are taxed and how distributions are made. An S corporation is a flow-through entity, meaning all the income, whether or not distributed, is taxed at the individual shareholder level. A C corporation can retain earnings and be taxed at both a corporate and individual level if there are dividend distributions. See also *business corporation, professional corporation.*

covered lives: The number of individual lives enrolled in a prepaid/capitated insurance plan serviced by the medical practice. A covered life is considered a member and is also known as an enrollee. A member is not considered a patient unless services are received during a particular month. (A covered life, enrollee, or member is one whose health care facility or provider receives monthly payments from the enrollee's insurance carrier.

Members become patients when services are rendered by their health care provider.)

CPT-4 code: *Physician's Current Procedural Terminology,* fourth edition, copyrighted by the American Medical Association.

current assets: Cash and other assets that are expected to be converted to cash, sold, or consumed in the normal course of operations within one year.

current liabilities: Liabilities that mature and require payment from current assets or through the creation of other liabilities within one year.

deferred revenue: Revenue received in one period applicable to services to be rendered in some future period.

deficit: The excess of expenses and other outflows over revenues and other inflows.

depreciation: As a general rule, depreciation is used to record the consumption or utilization over time of tangible property. Accumulated depreciation is a contra-account to the related fixed asset. Depreciation is recorded periodically, that is monthly, as an expense on the profit/loss or income statement earnings in the statement of operations. The offsetting entry is to increase (credit) accumulated depreciation.

donated capital: Increase in owners' equity due to assets contributed to the corporation.

donations: Any endowment or gift received by the organization.

encounter: An encounter includes only procedures from the evaluation and management chapter (CPT codes 99201–99499) or the medicine chapter (CPT codes 90800–99199) of the *Physician's Current Procedural Terminology,* fourth edition, copyrighted by the American Medical Association.

goodwill: Excess of costs over the fair market value of identifiable assets in the purchase of an entire organization.

grant revenue: Includes federal, state, or local government or private foundation grants to provide indigent patient care or case management of the frail and elderly.

gross charges: Established usual and customary rates are the full price for services before charge restrictions imposed by Medicare or contractual adjustments required by third-party payers, such as commercial insurance carriers or other adjustments. Services include all medical/surgical services provided by physicians and nonphysician providers as well as professional and technical components of ancillary services such as radiology and laboratory.

gross charges – FFS equivalents for capitation plan patients: Gross charges under capitation contracts for assigned enrollees under a patient care contract are recorded in this account. This account is used to record accrual basis revenues under risk-sharing arrangements such as bonuses and risk-pool allocations; however, the fees collected account series should be used to reflect revenues actually collected on these accounts.

group practice without walls (GPWW): A business entity formed by independent physicians or medical practices in order to create centralized management and decision-making structure and to share administrative, billing, and purchasing costs. The result is an organization with multiple sites. The physicians and medical practices retain their independence by maintaining their private offices and practice styles.

health maintenance organization (HMO): An insurance company indemnifies an insured party against a specified loss in return for premiums paid, as stipulated by a contract. An HMO, for-profit or not-for-profit, accepts responsibility for providing and delivering a predetermined set of comprehensive health maintenance and treatment services to a voluntarily enrolled population for a negotiated and fixed periodic premium.

income statement: A measure of the results of operations representing the difference between revenue and expense for the reported period. The income statement is used to summarize results of business operations for a period of time, not longer than one year, to determine whether the organization is operating efficiently.

incurred but not reported (IBNR): This liability represents claims that the organization is legally responsible to pay for services it has contracted with a managed care organization on a capitated basis and to subcontractors on a fee-for-service basis. It is an amount of money that the organization accrues for future medical expenses. These are medical expenses that the authorization system has not captured and for which claims have not yet been processed. IBNR can be calculated in a number of ways. The most common method is to track the history of claims payment for the specific organization to determine a claims' lag ratio and apply this ratio to current operations. IBNR can also be calculated actuarially based on anticipated utilization of a specific population. Another practical approach is to determine the number of referrals authorized but not billed as of a particular date and apply an average claim amount to these open referrals.

independent practice association/organization (IPA/IPO): An organization or network of licensed providers. This organization is a separate legal entity, usually operating on a for-profit basis. Typically, the primary purpose of the IPA/IPO is to secure and maintain contractual relationships between providers and health plans.

intangible assets: Property rights without physical substance that will benefit future operations of the organization. Intangible assets are purchased from external sources, provide future benefit, and are relatively long-lived. Other assets include long-term prepayments, deferred charges, goodwill, and assets not included in other categories.

interest expense: Interest incurred on borrowings.

interest income: Interest earned on marketable securities, certificates of deposit, savings accounts, and/or other short-term investments.

interest receivables: Interest that has been earned but not yet received.

investments – long-term receivables: Long-term investments in securities, property (not used for operations), and receivables due beyond one year. Assets recorded in these accounts will not be used to finance operations.

liabilities: Liabilities are debts or obligations owed by the organization to creditors. These debts arise as a result of the purchase of goods and services from others on credit and through cash borrowings to finance business operations. Liabilities are also obligations of responsibility to transfer other assets or to provide services to another entity.

limited liability company: A legal entity that is a hybrid between a corporation and a partnership; it provides limited liability to owners like a corporation, while passing profits and losses through to owners like a partnership.

long-term assets: Assets that are not expected to be converted to cash, sold, or otherwise consumed in the normal course of operations within one year.

long-term liabilities: Liabilities that will mature and require payment at some future time beyond one year.

malpractice insurance: Premiums or self-insurance cost for coverage of professional liability claims.

medical group: A medical practice consisting of at least three or more physicians who are engaged in the practice of medicine and share management and support staff personnel, facilities, equipment, and medical records.

medical practice: An organization consisting of at least one physician and/or nonphysician provider who delivers health care services. A medical practice does not need to be a single legal entity.

modified cash basis accounting: An accounting method that is primarily a cash basis system, as previously defined, but allows the cost of long-lived (fixed) assets to be expensed through depreciation. The modified cash system recognizes inventories of goods intended for resale as assets. Under a modified cash system, purchases of buildings and equipment, leasehold improvements, and payments of insurance premiums applicable to more than one accounting period are normally recorded as assets. Costs for these assets are allocated to accounting periods in a systematic manner over the length of time the practice benefits from the assets.

net assets: Excess of the not-for-profit entity's assets over its liabilities. The balances in these accounts are the cumulative results of original investments, grants, gifts, donations, and revenues and expenditures.

noncurrent expenses paid in advance: Costs incurred (payments) for goods or services that will benefit future operations (beyond a year).

nonoperating revenues: Revenues not directly related to patient care or the provision of medical services.

nonphysician providers: Specially trained and licensed nonphysician providers (also known as physician extenders), employed or contracted, who can provide medical care and bill for services without continuous supervision by a physician.

notes payable – long-term: Notes payable that mature more than one year from financial statement date. The current portion of any long-term liability should be included in "long-term debt – current portion," except those obligations to be refinanced or paid from a sinking fund.

notes receivable – short-term: Amounts owed to the organization by other entities where the obligation is represented by a note having a maturity of one year or less.

not-for-profit entity: A legal entity that has obtained special exemption under Section 501(c) of the Internal Revenue Code that qualifies the organization to be exempt from federal income taxes. To qualify as a tax-exempt organization, an entity, practice, or faculty practice plan has to provide advance evidence of a planned charitable, educational, or research purpose.

occupancy expense: Expenses related to the occupancy and use of land and buildings. In the event that another legal entity owns the land or buildings, any rental fees, commissions or charges paid to the other entity are charged to this account. For the purpose of peer comparison (e.g., comparative data or cost survey), a fair market rental value may be charged to this account even if no rent is otherwise charged to the organization by the owning entity.

operating expenses: Expired costs incurred in the process of providing medical services to the organization's patients. Excludes all costs pertaining to nonoperating activities such as general investments and endowments.

organization costs: Costs incurred in the original incorporation and start-up of a business operation. These costs are generally amortized over a period of five years.

owners' equity: A residual interest or claim of the owners to the assets after creditor claims are settled. (Legally, creditors are first in line to receive reimbursement.) Owners' equity derives from two sources:

1. Contributed capital, which is the investment of cash or other assets by the owner or owners; and/or

2. Retained earnings, the accumulative results of income, less losses and withdrawals over the years.

partnership: A legal entity where two or more individuals have agreed that they will share profits and losses and assets and liabilities, although not necessarily on an equal basis. The partnership agreement is typically formalized in writing.

patient: A unique patient is one who is counted only once per month, regardless of the number of times that patient sees a specific physician or nonphysician provider. This patient count is per physician or nonphysician provider. If the patient sees more than one physician or nonphysician provider during a certain month, each physician or nonphysician provider receives a patient count of one. If the patient does not receive any services during a particular month, the patient is not counted in that month's total patients.

patient refunds: Refunds of amounts collected from patients that should not have been collected or that need to be returned for some other reason. The corresponding credit is cash or accounts payable. This account should be used only if the specific revenue in which the payment was originally recorded is not used.

payroll tax withholdings payable: Actual liabilities for payroll tax withholdings. These accounts are credited (increased) for amounts withheld from employees and are debited (decreased) when payment is made to the appropriate agency, authority, or plan.

permanently restricted net assets: Net assets with donor restrictions that do not expire with the passage of time and cannot be removed by any actions taken by the medical organization other than for its restricted use. Endowment funds are an example.

preferred provider organization (PPO): Independent health care providers that contract with a managed care plan to provide services at a discount. PPOs may or may not be risk-bearing entities.

preferred stock: A type of stock whose holders are given certain priority over common stockholders in the payment of dividends and liquidation/termination of the entity. Usually the dividend rate is fixed at the time of stock issue.

prepaid expenses: Payments for goods or services that will benefit future operations.

procedure code: Typically the Current Procedural Terminology (CPT-4) code performed by a provider, but it could also be a home-grown or other recognized code from the McGraw-Hill scale, for instance. In Physician Services Practice Analysis CPT download files, these codes are associated with the provider that performed them.

professional corporation: A legal entity whose shareholders must typically all be licensed to practice in the same profession as that practiced by the organization. State law determines whether all shareholders must be licensed.

realized gains and losses – investments: Gains or losses recognized on closed and sold securities during the period.

relative value unit (RVU): A nonmonetary standard unit of measure that indicates the value of services provided by physicians, non-physician providers, and other health care professionals.

resource-based relative value scale (RBRVS): Developed by the Health Care Financing Administration for use by Medicare. Relative values are assigned to each CPT-4 code based on the amount of resources used to provide a given service.

retained earnings – appropriated: Restrictions placed on portions of earnings retained in the corporation. These restrictions may temporarily limit the amount of dividends available for distribution to owners. This account should be used to record the creation of unfunded reserves required by state health maintenance organization laws or regulations.

retained earnings – unappropriated: Net income (or loss) over the life of the corporation minus all distributions to owners and appropriations of retained earnings carried in the retained earnings – appropriated account.

revenue and expense summary: A summary account for use in the closing of revenue and expense accounts when financial statements are prepared.

revenues: Inflows of cash and other items of value received or to be received for services rendered. There are different measures of these inflows of cash for fee-for-service (FFS) revenues, depending on whether the organization identifies gross charges, adjustments, and allowances; whether the organization uses the cash,

modified cash, or accrual basis of accounting; and whether a
prepaid plan pays discounted FFS or capitation.

risk-sharing revenues: Any mechanism that gives incentive to providers to render cost-effective, high-quality health care.

stockholders' equity: Net assets of the corporation; that is, the excess
of the corporate entity's assets over its liabilities. The balances in
these accounts are the cumulative result of the owners' investments and the equity originating from net earnings retained by
the corporation.

surplus: The excess of revenues and other inflows over expenses and
other outflows.

unrealized gains and losses – investments: The accounting recognition
of the difference between the fair market value of carried investments and the adjusted cost (current "book" value) of those
investments for the period.

unrestricted net assets: Unrestricted equity of the not-for-profit entity.
Equity resulting from incurring revenues for providing or agreeing to provide health care services, receiving unrestricted contributions and/or grants, or receiving dividend or interest from
investing in income-producing assets minus expenses incurred
in providing or agreeing to provide health care services or other
community benefits and performing administrative functions.

withhold: A percentage of the primary care capitation rate that is
withheld every month and used to cover the cost overruns
(excess medical expenses) in referral or organizational services.
Typically used in capitation contracts or other risk-sharing
arrangements, this account is reconciled at year-end. If the entire
amount of the withhold was not required to cover cost overruns,
the remainder may be distributed or kept in the account to fund
the risk pool as determined by contract terms.

Index

Note: (ex.) indicates exhibit.